MIT Press Series on the Regulation of Economic Activity

General Editor
Richard Schmalensee, MIT Sloan School of Management

1 *Freight Transport Regulation*, Ann F. Friedlaender and Richard H. Spady, 1980

2 *The SEC and the Public Interest*, Susan M. Phillips and J. Richard Zecher, 1981

The SEC and the Public Interest

This book was set in VIP Times Roman by DEKR Corporation and printed and bound by The Murray Printing Company in the United States of America.

Library of Congress Cataloging in Publication Data

Phillips, Susan M., 1944–
    The SEC and the public interest.

    (MIT Press series on the regulation of economic activity ; 2)
    Bibliography: p.
    Includes index.
    1. United States.   Securities and Exchange Commission.   I. Zecher, J. Richard.   II. Title.
III. Series.
KF1444.P5   346.73′0666   81-4491
ISBN 0-262-16080-3   347.306666   AACR2

The SEC and the Public Interest

Susan M. Phillips
and J. Richard Zecher

The MIT Press
Cambridge, Massachusetts, and London, England

Contents

Series Foreword   vii

Acknowledgments   ix

Introduction   1

Chapter 1   Historical Perspectives of the SEC   5

   1.1   Historical Development of Capital Market Regulation   5

   1.2   The Purposes of the Securities and Exchange Commission   8

   1.3   The Regulatory Evolution of the SEC   12

   1.4   Summary   15

Chapter 2   Economic Theories of Regulation   17

   2.1   Market Failure Theory of Regulation   18

   2.2   Public Choice Theory of Regulation   21

   2.3   Comparison of the Two Theories   24

Chapter 3   Corporate Disclosure   27

   3.1   Pricing Efficiency and Corporate Disclosure   29

   3.2   Equal Access to Corporate Information and Corporate Disclosure   36

   3.3   The Relationship between Owners and Managers and Corporate Disclosure   37

   3.4   Estimated Costs of SEC Corporate Disclosure   42

   3.5   Estimated Costs of Filing 10-K, 10-Q, and 8-K   44

   3.6   Estimated Costs of SEC New Issue Disclosure   46

   3.7   A Comparison of Voluntary and SEC-Mandated Periodic Disclosure Costs   49

   3.8   Summary   49

Chapter 4   Deregulation of the NYSE Fixed Commission
Rate Structure   53

4.1 Background   53

4.2 Public Choice Theory of Regulation   60

4.3 Empirical Test of the Transfer Tax in the
Public Choice Theory of Regulation   64

4.4 The Producer Groups in the Provision of
Execution Services   84

4.5 Summary   87

Chapter 5   Market Structure   91

5.1 Background of the Market Structure for
the Trading of Securities   92

5.2 Exchange Seats as Capital Assets   101

5.3 The Future of the Regional Exchanges   107

5.4 Summary   109

Chapter 6   Conclusions   111

6.1 Corporate Disclosure   112

6.2 Deregulation of the NYSE Fixed
Commission Rate Structure   114

6.3 Market Structure   116

6.4 Future Directions of the SEC   118

Appendixes

A Deregulation Calculations   121

B Yearly Changes in Exchange Seat Prices   141

C Comparison of NYSE and Phlx Seat Prices   153

Notes   157

References   165

Bibliography   167

Index   175

Series Foreword

Government regulation of economic activity in the United States has grown dramatically in this century, radically transforming government-business relations. Economic regulation of prices and conditions of service was first applied to transportation and public utilities and has recently been extended in energy, health care, and other sectors. In the 1970s, explosive growth occurred in social regulation focusing on workplace safety, environmental preservation, consumer protection, and related goals. The expansion of regulation has not proceeded in silence. Critics have argued that many regulatory programs produce negative net benefits, while regulation's defenders have pointed to the sound rationales for and potential gains from many of the same programs.

The purpose of the MIT Press series on Regulation of Economic Activity is to inform the ongoing debate on regulatory policy by making significant and relevant research available to both scholars and decision makers. The books in this series will present new insights into individual agencies, programs, and regulated sectors, as well as the important economic, political, and administrative aspects of the regulatory process that cut across these boundaries.

This study of the Securities and Exchange Commission by J. Richard Zecher and Susan M. Phillips uses the tools of both financial and regulatory economics to analyze the activities and effects of an important New Deal agency that has received surprisingly little scholarly attention. Zecher and Phillips challenge the conventional presumption that the commission's corporate disclosure program serves the public interest. They find substantial costs and no tangible net benefits from this program. In addition, they analyze the political economy of the deregulation of fixed commission rates and of the commission's impact on the evolution of a national market system for trading common stocks. The analysis is enriched by considerable interesting and original empirical work and by the presentation of an informed historical and institutional perspective. Those interested in capital markets as well as those interested in the general properties of the regulatory process will learn a great deal from this volume.

Richard Schmalensee

Acknowledgments

This volume has benefited in many ways from colleagues and friends. We owe a major debt of gratitude to Roderick Hills, former chairman of the Securities and Exchange Commission who, incredible as it may sound, encouraged independent economic research of actual SEC policy issues. Of the many SEC staff members from whom we learned, we would like to single out Lee A. Pichard, Esq., former director of the Division of Market Regulation, who was and is ever willing to learn and to teach, and William Dale, who helped us on our early work on the unfixing of commission rates. Four graduate students at The University of Iowa contributed greatly to the empirical aspects of the book: James Tully worked on the corporate disclosure chapter; Kim Korn worked mainly on the unfixing of commission rates; Joseph Cole mainly on market structure; and Dan Roberts, who worked on everything, also co-authored with us a paper on the unfixing of commission rates. We would also like to thank those who read and commented on the manuscript, including Fisher Black, George Benston, Richard Schmalensee, Michael Mann, Donald McCloskey, James Bush, as well as Robert Soldofsky and other members of the Finance Workshop at The University of Iowa. Last but far from least, we would like to thank Margaret Helble for typing most of the many drafts of the manuscript, and Linda Grandchamp, who also provided typing assistance during the hectic final months of revisions.

The SEC and the Public Interest

Introduction

Each proposed new regulation should be examined in the light of available economic evidence before being adopted. Monitoring programs should be created to permit us to determine later whether or not regulations we adopt are producing the result we expected. . . .

We must instill in our regulators an appreciation of the therapeutic value of competition and a willingness to temper the lawyers' urge to regulate relentlessly with economic data that tests the need for regulation. Skeptics have warned me that our effort to improve the Commission's capacity for economic analysis rests on a misplaced confidence in the ability of economists. But I am confident that our efforts to improve our economic capability will be worth it, if only the influence of the lawyers and the economists cancel each other out.

SEC Chairman Roderick M. Hills (May 26, 1976)

A full understanding of securities regulation would encompass all types of regulatory activities that have been occurring since the inception of securities markets in the late eighteenth century. It would therefore be misleading to attach too much significance to a single episode such as the founding of the Securities and Exchange Commission (SEC) in the depths of the Great Depression. While the event brought the full power of the federal government to the enforcement of the rules and regulations that already governed the issuance and trading of securities and contracts between managers and owners of corporations, those rules and regulations had been developing for about 150 years and may not have evolved in any significantly different way if the SEC had been founded 100 years earlier (or later, for that matter). The market forces leading to the development of the earlier rules, and to the founding of exchanges and other organizations to enforce them, still may operate through the mechanisms of the SEC.

This is not to suggest that the existence of the SEC makes no difference, that the form of the rules would be precisely the same without the SEC, or that the enforcement of those rules through the power of law as compared to the use of market sanctions is unimportant. Rules and regulations promulgated in Washington might differ somewhat from those initiated by private organizations such as stock exchanges since the relative power of interest groups is stronger or weaker there and since different interest groups would become involved in the process. We believe, however, that the difference between SEC-initiated and, for example, exchange-initiated rules is one of form or emphasis and not one of substance: the rules would exist with or without the SEC (and perhaps more cheaply without).

The primary argument for moving the rule-making function from the private sector to Washington was to protect and enhance the interests of a group alleged to have little power in the market sector, namely, the widows-and-orphans group of small investors. Whether moving the rulemaking function out of the private sector to Washington has actually helped this group remains, in our minds, a very open question.

There is less question that the enforcement of rules, using the full power of the federal law, has wrought some changes in the regulation of securities markets. Undeniably the legalization of securities regulation has created an important new interest group composed of securities lawyers and, to a lesser extent so far, financial accountants. About one-third of the SEC's approximately 2,000 employees are lawyers. They interact mainly with former and future lawyer colleagues who represent the thousands of registered corporations, the hundreds of brokerage firms and investment companies, and the regulated exchanges and professional organizations. The interests of this group are sometimes different from the interests of other groups in the securities markets, including those of widows and orphans, and have undoubtedly had some impact on which rules are adopted and how they are enforced. It is also significant that in recent years the SEC has come under increasing criticism for being a costly agency with doubtful benefits to the public. The strongest defenders (as well as some of the attackers) of the commission have come from the ranks of securities lawyers.

In this book we take an economist's approach to analyzing the SEC and its programs. Our primary emphasis is on the effect this agency has on the allocation of resources and how the groups affected by these reallocations determine the evolution and enforcement of the new rules. To set the stage for this analysis, we review the history of stock exchanges and the SEC in chapter 1. While the vigor of the SEC has waxed and waned several times over its fifty-year history, today it is responsible for allocating well in excess of one billion dollars of resources per year, probably differently than they would be allocated in an unregulated market. Further, it seems to expand its role both in traditional areas such as corporate disclosure and in newer areas relating to the structure of markets for securities.

Chapter 2 is devoted to introducing the economics of regulation. One general economic approach sets a welfare standard for regulation, asserting that regulation should be undertaken only if (1) there is a clear failure in the marketplace, (2) the proposed regulation alleviates the failure without generating other serious problems, and (3) the costs of the regulation to society are in balance with the benefits. A second general approach to regulation takes the much more pessimistic, and perhaps also more realistic, view that regulation simply relfects the relative power of competing interest groups. Winning groups (those most powerful) succeed in taxing losing groups (the less powerful), and the resulting regulatory frame has little to do with correcting failures in the marketplace.

In chapter 3 we examine the major and most costly program of the SEC, its corporate disclosure system. We review the rationale for this program and examine the available evidence to ascertain if and to what extent the disclosure system achieves its stated purposes. We also examine data on the costs of this program and conclude that the costs appear to far outweigh the benefits, if any, to society.

We turn in chapter 4 to a major example of deregulation, the removal of fixed commission rates. Our approach here is to examine how the economic interests of various groups in the fixed commission structure changed over the period when rates were deregulated. We find persuasive evidence to support the notion that the unfixing of rates and the timing for that deregulatory action are consistent with sharp increases in economic incentives for some groups to oppose fixed rates and lessened incentives for other groups to support them. In a word, this deregulatory episode can be explained by changes in the marketplace to which the rule makers and law makers in Washington responded almost in a passive manner.

In chapter 5 we turn to issues of market structure, which have come to be subsumed under the rubric of the national market system. The 1975 amendments to the securities acts among other things gave the SEC the mandate to facilitate a national market system. The SEC was to help perfect this system in some unspecified way. Some observers feel that this mandate is equivalent to handing the conductor's baton to the SEC and specifying which symphony is to be performed. In our view a more accurate analogy would be to a jazz improvisation, where the leads are played by the same important interest groups that have determined major regulatory changes in the past. The chances of even an harmonic composition are dim, to say the least.

We come away from this experience with the feeling that the SEC is both less powerful and more costly than is commonly believed. Its primary role seems to be to referee the competing demands of interest groups and more significantly, to create or nurture an artifice—an interest group of experts in securities regulations. From this point of view the observation that SEC rules do not alter market realities very much should not surprise: there are powerful market interests devoted to this end; and the observation that regulation seems excessively costly also should not surprise: there are powerful interests to assure that these regulations, effective or not, are at least very costly to administer.

Chapter 1

Historical Perspectives of the SEC

Of all the New Deal agencies created in Franklin Roosevelt's first term, none began life with more publicity, interest and glamour than did the SEC. In these respects, it could be compared to the congressional committees investigating Watergate corruption and considering impeachment. Roosevelt had come to office at the bottom of the worst depression in American history and the nation's greatest crisis since the Civil War. The public already had its scapegoat—Wall Street—and was convinced the bad times had been signalled by the Great Crash of October, 1929. The public demanded action, by way of punishment and reforms. F.D.R. was prepared to offer both.

Robert Sobel, *Inside Wall Street* (New York: Norton, 1977), p. 167.

The SEC is widely regarded as one of the more prestigious and effective of the federal regulatory agencies. Its broad charge of protecting investors and maintaining fair and orderly markets grew out of the stock market crash of 1929 and the perception that fraud, security price manipulation, short selling, bear raids, pooling, and other unsavory investment practices were the root of the ensuing Great Depression. The nation needed a scapegoat, and Wall Street was an attractive candidate. The SEC, which actually was not launched until nearly five years after the crash, was perceived by the public as the mechanism that would offer protection against unscrupulous inside traders and security issuers and perhaps even against future security losses.

The period immediately following the stock market crash brought considerable debate as to the necessity and form of any federal security regulation. The final product actually was the result of several evolutionary efforts to develop capital market regulation, and the compromises reflect not only the historical role of security regulation but also the tenor of the times and the political beliefs of the major characters for formulating the regulations.

1.1 Historical Development of Capital Market Regulation

Before the SEC came onto the scene, participants in the markets had developed their own, fairly elaborate version of self regulation: the exchange system. The trading of securities in the late 1700s and through the early 1900s was a function of the existing communication and information systems. Because of the costs of such communication networks and the early accumulation of wealth in New York, Philadelphia, and Boston, the trading of stocks and bonds tended to be concentrated in those areas. Traders simply congregated together to execute stock transactions and soon developed formalized exchange rules to govern the charges for executing trades, the traders' conduct, and specifications of exchange trades. The earliest such agreement was the famous Buttonwood Tree Agreement, to which the New York Stock Exchange (NYSE) traces its roots. On May 17, 1792, a group of twenty-four traders signed the following agreement under that famous tree:

We the undersigned, brokers for the purchase and sale of public stocks, do hereby promise and pledge ourselves to each other that we will not buy or sell from this date for any person whatever, any kind of public stocks at less rate than one quarter of one percent commission on the specie value, and that we will give preference to each other in our negotiations.

The two basic premises of that agreement, fixed commissions and trading priorities to members, have historically characterized all exchange rules in one form or another. These principles remained unchallenged until the 1970s when the SEC at the direction of Congress deregulated commission rates and began the movement toward a national market system.

The first major external regulatory structure governing the capital markets was that initiated by the individual states. Massachusetts enacted legislation in the 1850s, and other states followed with additional "blue sky laws." All of this legislation was centered around control of new issues and often was implemented through the state chartering of corporations. Blue sky laws never attempted to regulate or influence the trading of existing securities, although some states (most notably New York) did institute a tax on all transactions effected in that state.

The second major type of legislation that affected the issuance and trading of stocks and bonds was the antitrust legislation. The trust-busting era of the early 1900s affected not only the issuance of new securities but also the formation of new corporations. The concern about corporate monopolies, which began in the late 1800s and resulted in the elaborate antitrust regulatory structure in the Justice Department, consistently has been a central theme of security or capital market regulation. Even the SEC, when it came on the regulatory scene, was given some duties in this area for specialized kinds of corporations—public utility holding companies.

Aside from the state blue sky laws and the federal regulation of antitrust laws, there was little formal regulation of the securities markets prior to the SEC. In particular little attempt was made to regulate either the secondary trading of stocks and bonds or the disclosure of financial information in any consistent manner or on a national basis. These areas were left to the private sector and increasingly to the emerging self-regulatory bodies.

Although there was little government regulation of the trading of securities or the disclosure of financial information prior to the SEC, there was a growing demand in the private sector for establishing and enforcing certain rules and codes of conduct. A wide range of self-regulatory bodies met these demands, including the stock exchanges already mentioned, national organizations of brokers like the National Association of Securities Dealers or the Put and Call Dealers Association which governed nonexchange trades, and various accounting organizations. Some of the roles of these self-regulatory organizations included setting and enforcing codes of conduct in dealing with the public, setting and enforcing fee structures, and determining accounting and other standards of corporate disclosure to the public.

With the establishment of the SEC government oversight of the self-regulatory bodies was introduced. The major responsibilities of the commission fall into two areas that have their bases in the historical development of capital market regulation. First, the commission was most active in assuming control of the corporate disclosure programs of the self-regulatory bodies, via oversight of accounting organizations and exchanges. The federal regulations in the area have far surpassed the state blue sky laws or exchange issuer disclosure requirements in importance. The expansion and enforcement of these accounting procedures have remained a major activity of the SEC to the present day. The second major activity that the SEC assumed concerned establishing and enforcing codes of conduct for brokers and dealers, particularly with respect to fraud and stock price manipulation, once left completely to exchanges and broker-dealer organizations.

1.2   The Purposes of the Securities and Exchange Commission

At the time of the stock market crash in 1929 and the alleged loss of investor confidence in the securities markets, the range of proposed legislation in the area of securities and securities markets was broad, ranging from complete government control of the markets to something close to complete laissez faire. As with many legislative initiatives, the final result was a compromise, and the commission itself has developed and changed its focus over the years.

Herbert Hoover, who was president during the years of the stock market crash and the beginning of the depression, in spite of strong public sentiment consistently avoided initiatives to regulate the securities market, claiming that the private institutions and states should govern themselves. He maintained that state blue sky laws which governed corporation chartering and security issuance were the appropriate arm for security and market regulation and wondered whether federal regulation could even be authorized under our Constitution.

When the exchanges did not appear to be willing to take strong oversight initiatives, and stock market abuses continued to make headlines, Hoover finally appealed directly to the exchanges, Richard Whitney, head of the NYSE, in particular, to eliminate manipulation and restrict trader activities on exchange floors. Whitney was an eloquent defender of the freedom of the marketplace and the NYSE's role in the maintenance of the integrity of the market. In 1931, after the NYSE failed to take measures in response to Hoover's expressed dissatisfaction, Hoover initiated a Senate investigation. That investigation continued through 1932 and the presidential election and produced numerous headlines about security manipulations, bucket shops, stock watering, and short-selling bear raids. The Senate committee's findings of fraud and abuse formed the foundation of a Democratic plank, advocating federal regulation of holding companies, public utilities, and security and commodity exchanges.

Federal regulation of securities was an interesting campaign issue for the 1932 presidential race because Hoover's opponent, Franklin D. Roosevelt, was the governor of New York, the state in which many of the alleged abuses were occurring and, as Hoover was quick to point out, states were responsible for security and exchange regulation. Hoover generally took the tact that specific wrongdoings should be punished and that there was doubtful authority for federal regulation of securities under the Constitution. The Roosevelt New Deal approach which had a flower of experimentation with concrete remedies, particularly in the areas of business and finance, seemed to win over the American public, and the mandate for securities regulation coming out of the 1932 election was clear. FDR's proposals for wide-ranging banking and finance regulation could be implemented with the blessing of the American public.

Roosevelt's first securities regulatory reform bill which called for the regulation of securities by the Federal Trade Commission (FTC) was introduced in both Houses in March 1933. Although the bill was subject to considerable debate and was modified somewhat before it was finally signed on May 27, 1933, the Securities Act of 1933 was substantially as Roosevelt had suggested and was billed as a part of the long-term development of a regulatory program for securities.

By passing the 1933 act, sometimes called the truth-in-securities law, Congress opted for a disclosure approach to securities regulation: issuers of securities were required to disclose the financial underpinnings of stock and bond issues. It was believed that disclosure in the glaring light of publicity would provide investors with sufficient information to be able to make informed investment decisions that would serve to self-regulate the allocation of capital. This concept was implemented through the registration of securities with and administration by the FTC. The 1933 act has two basic purposes: to provide investors with sufficient material information to enable informed investment decisions and to prohibit fraud in connection with the sale of securities. The disclosure and antifraud provisions of the 1933 act remain a central focus of federal security regulation today.

One year later, and even while the FTC was beginning the administration of the 1933 act, Roosevelt continued his quest of regulating the financial markets by addressing the regulation of the trading of existing securities (as opposed to the regulation of the primary market which is covered by the 1933 act). Regulation of existing securities would encompass exchanges, broker-dealer activities, and even investor activities.

Roosevelt appointed a committee, headed by Secretary of Commerce Daniel C. Roper, to examine the need for and form of a regulatory structure for stock and commodity markets. The Roper report recommended a very mild form of exchange regulation, basically the federal registration and licensing of exchanges and the formation of a new agency. The report even recommended that the administration of the new agency be drawn from the staff of the stock exchanges since security regulation would involve considerable technical expertise. Although the Roper report recommended a mild dose of federal regulation, the bills introduced in both Houses were much stronger and showed the influence of several congressional committees that advocated more stringent exchange-regulation and oversight by the FTC. For example, the Senate version was drafted by Ferdinand Pecora, counsel for the Senate Banking and Currency Committee which was investigating exchange practices and producing a number of headlines related to investment banking and exchange practices.

Wall Street mounted a massive campaign against the congressional versions of the bill, arguing that the FTC would be able to control all corporations, that nationalization of all industry surely would result, and that the demise of capital markets and capital formation was imminent. Roosevelt firmly supported the strong congressional bills and FTC oversight. In an effort to stave off perceived disaster, Wall Street then argued for a separate agency, hoping to develop friendly ties in the fledgling regulatory agency.

The final bill which was passed as the Securities Exchange Act of 1934 did call for a separate agency, but no other concessions were made. In fact Roosevelt seems to have lost little when the scope and composition of the new commission is examined. Roosevelt's initial appointees included three people from the FTC (James M. Landis, George M. Matthews, and Robert E. Healy), Ferdinand Pecora (one of the drafters of the bill), and Joseph Kennedy as chairman. With the exception of the appointment of Kennedy, Wall Street could take little comfort in the formation of a new separate agency. In fact most of the securities division of the FTC was transferred directly over to the SEC.

The early years of the SEC were devoted to taking over the administration of the 1933 act and carrying out the mandate of the 1934 act. The major requirements of the 1934 act include registration of securities traded on national exchanges, certain periodic financial reports of those securities, registration of exchanges and broker-dealers, antifraud provisions, prohibitions against wash sales (allegedly no-risk sales with repurchase agreements to create the illusion of volume and investor interest), standards for transactions among managers, board members, and others with nonpublic material information (called insiders), proxy solicitation, and tender offer solicitations and enforcement of margin credit restrictions imposed by the Federal Reserve

Board. In 1938 the Malony act extended the 1934 act to cover the over-the-counter (OTC) market and the regulation of qualified broker-dealer associations. Although the registration of exchanges resulted in the closing of nine exchanges (including a one-person exchange in a poolroom in Hammond, Indiana), the early years of the SEC were marked by Kennedy's speeches and efforts to support and encourage the mainstream of the flagging financial markets. He touted the SEC's better business bureau role and suggested that the SEC could protect the honest exchanges, traders, and investors from the fraudulent dealers.

The SEC quickly established itself as a reputable and reasonable regulatory agency under the leadership of Kennedy and as such was soon the recipient of additional regulatory powers. One of Roosevelt's strongest personal public service interests, dating even before his days as governor of the state of New York, lay in the area of power and public utility holding companies. Roosevelt believed that electricity was of such vital importance to everyone that control over that resource meant virtual control over the public's money. Such power, he believed, should not be concentrated in powerful corporate entities. A study of public utilities by the FTC had been ordered under the Coolidge administration, and it was completed in early 1935 under the direction of Robert E. Healy, the general counsel of the FTC, who later came over to the SEC as a commissioner. The report, the well-known desire of Roosevelt to curb utility power, and the widely perceived popularity of controlling the monopoly power of the public utilities soon combined to produce several versions of public utility holding company bills in Congress, all of which called for the death sentence of the holding companies.

When the import of the bills was widely understood, the utilities and Wall Street began a strong and active lobby campaign to block passage and even enlisted the support of the shareholders who believed that the death sentence would erode their stock values. Congress found itself caught in the middle and sought the safe harbor of requiring utility holding company disclosure, keeping the death sentence in the bill, but making the SEC the arbiter.

The Public Holding Company Act of 1935 also contained a mandate for the SEC to study the functions and activities of investment trust and investment companies. The reports submitted to Congress formed the basis for the Trust Indenture Act of 1939, the Investment Company Act of 1940, and the Investment Advisors Act of 1940. The Trust

Indenture Act requires that publicly traded debt securities be issued only under a SEC-approved trust indenture and only when a trustee meeting certain minimum requirements is appointed. The two acts passed in 1940 govern the registration and disclosure of investment companies and advisers, prevent fraud in connection with investment companies and advisers, and define certain prohibited transactions. The registration/disclosure themes of all three of these acts are similar to the regulatory modes established in the 1933 and 1934 acts, although the three later acts have never achieved the same levels of importance as the first two enabling acts for the SEC.

1.3   The Regulatory Evolution of the SEC

As a result of both a number of congressional mandates and the interests of some of the early chairmen, a number of studies were undertaken by the SEC. Joe Kennedy and James Landis who succeeded Kennedy as chairman after only fifteen months persuaded William O. Douglas, one of the drafters of the 1933 act and a respected law professor at Yale, to head a study of corporate reorganization. That study was to be the basis for Chapter IX Bankruptcy legislation, under which the SEC acts as an advisor to the courts. At the same time the SEC staff studied investment companies, trust indentures, and the governance of stock exchanges. As mentioned earlier, the first two studies resulted in recommended legislation, but the latter report was submitted to Congress and recommended that no further legislation was needed for the proper regulation of the exchanges. By that recommendation the SEC reinforced its role as a disclosure and anti-fraud agency, not as a regulatory arm to restructure the marketplace. The SEC was to correct specific wrongs and maintain fair and orderly markets, not disrupt or reorganize the basic functionings of the capital markets.

It is interesting to note that the NYSE underwent some reorganization and reform in the late 1930s at the initiation of NYSE members and under the prodding of the SEC's third chairman, William O. Douglas. Chairman Douglas virtually threatened the NYSE with a SEC takeover if reforms were not instituted. Grudgingly the NYSE undertook a reorganizational effort that was speeded by an internal scandal. Richard Whitney, the leader of the old guard of the exchange actually was indicted for misappropriation of securities belonging to the NYSE pension trust fund. Reformers within the exchange were

Table 1.1 The changing size of the Securities and Exchange Commission

	Number of personnel[a]	SEC budget as a percent of total federal outlays
1935	369	0.0233
1936	879	0.0352
1937	1,121	0.0474
1940	1,587	0.0594
1945	1,130	0.0046
1950	1,062	0.0149
1955	692	0.0070
1960	952	0.0088
1965	1,393	0.0129
1970	1,388	0.0109
1975	1,911	0.0136
1976	1,987	0.0138
1977	1,912	0.0133
1978	1,955[b]	0.0137
1979	2,015[b]	na

Sources: *Report of the Secretary of the Treasury,* 1978, pp. 10–12; *Budget of the U.S. Government,* various years.
[a]On account of the data available, before 1945 the number of authorized positions is reported, and for the later years the average number of employees is reported.
[b]Estimated.

able to accomplish considerable reforms. Further market declines in the late 1930s hardly made Wall Street a likely candidate for reform by zealous SEC regulators. Douglas resigned to take a seat on the Supreme Court in 1939. He was the last of the early influential leaders of the SEC.

Throughout the 1940s and 1950s the SEC almost disappeared from the regulatory scene, losing both budget and employees during the period, see table 1.1. After its dramatic growth in the 1930s and even with new regulatory responsibilities to administer in the 1940s, the SEC actually shrank until the 1960s. A staff of 1,600 in 1940 shrank to slightly over 1,000 by 1950 and to 690 in 1955. The agency was moved to Philadelphia during World War II and may not even have been missed. A series of chairmen during that period were hardly notable, and the SEC itself became known as the toothless tiger and a training ground for Wall Street securities lawyers.

The election of John F. Kennedy in 1960 coincided with the climax of a stock manipulation scandal on the Amex. Kennedy asked former SEC Chairman Landis to prepare a report on the regulatory commissions. Completed late in 1960, the report was particularly critical of the SEC. Kennedy asked Congress to fund and oversee a special study of the securities markets. The special study completed in 1963, under the direction of Milton Cohen, resulted in the Securities Act Amendments of 1964 which extended the disclosure requirements of the securities of companies that trade over the counter, created more stringent standards for broker-dealers, and gave the SEC new powers to regulate the markets.

The special study and Kennedy's first chairman, William Cary, seemed to give the SEC new life, a revival in the New Deal tradition, but the weakness of the market in 1962 caused some moderation in the Kennedy-Cary reform effort. The SEC chairman under Johnson, Manuel Cohen, concentrated on enforcement and tended to ignore market regulation issues. President Nixon's first chairman, Hamer Budge, generally was regarded as pro-NYSE and did little to pursue regulatory reform despite exchange back office problems, financial failures of commission houses, demands for deregulation of fixed commission rates, challenges from the third market for market restructuring, and pressure from congressional oversight committees. The Securities Investor Protection Act (SIPA) of 1970 was passed by Congress to respond to the paper crunch problems and commission house failures in the late 1960s. Under Budge the SEC was viewed as so weak that, when the SIPA of 1970 was passed, a separate corporation was set up to protect investors outside of the SEC authority: the Securities Investor Protection Corporation.

The next two chairmen appointed by Nixon did little to change the direction of the SEC. William J. Casey restored the morale of the staff and encouraged their efforts to deregulate commission rates. G. Bradford Cook got caught up in Watergate improprieties and resigned after two and a half months in office. Ray Garrett, however, reasserted SEC leadership, encouraged more aggressive enforcement actions by Stanley Sporkin, chief of the Enforcement Division, and helped guide through Congress the 1975 amendments to the securities acts. Most of these amendments were to the Securities Exchange Act of 1934 and mandated the SEC, among other things, to eliminate anticompetitive exchange rules, deregulate commission rates, and facilitate the development of a national market system. The commission is still in the process of trying to carry out these mandates.

Roderick Hills, who was appointed by President Ford, initiated a massive reexamination of the corporate disclosure requirements, under the direction of former Commissioner Albert A. Sommers. Hills also encouraged the developments of the fledgling stock options markets, and continued to carry out the mandates of the 1975 amendments, including fixed commission rate deregulation and facilitation of the development of the national market system. His tenure was less than two years, and many of his projects were left uncompleted. Chairman Harold Williams who was appointed by President Carter has discouraged the growth of the options markets, but it may be too early to discuss the influence of his chairmanship on the direction of the SEC.

1.4 Summary

The SEC, which came out of Roosevelt's New Deal, saw a burst of energy in the 1930s. The young agency, under the direction of such regulatory conservatives as Joe Kennedy, James Landis, and William O. Douglas developed a regulatory philosophy that pervades all of its jurisdictions. SEC regulation has as its central principles full disclosure, antifraud provisions, and self-regulation. The most important of the SEC acts today remain those first passed in 1933 and 1934.

The commission has throughout its tradition been expanded as the result of congressional or SEC staff studies. We find ourselves at a possible watershed for the future of the SEC. On the one hand, the SEC has successfully overseen the deregulation of the NYSE fixed commission rates, as mandated by the 1975 amendments. But, on the other hand, the national market system as mandated by these amendments seems far from determined, and some would say has foundered. In a similar vein the disclosure report begun under the leadership of Chairman Hills has not produced any cries for massive regulatory reform, as has often been the case with previous commission studies. Rather the premises of the original disclosure philosophy have not changed, and the basic message of the disclosure report is that we should expand the disclosure system.

Why do we observe these three very different regulatory phenomena in such an established regulatory agency? Before we can address these questions, a theoretical framework of regulation must be developed to allow a careful economic analysis of disclosure, fixed commission rates, and market structure.

Chapter 2

Economic Theories of Regulation

> The essential commodity being transacted in the political market is a transfer of wealth, with constituents on the demand side and their political representatives on the supply side. Viewed in this way, the market here, as elsewhere, will distribute more of the good to those whose effective demand is highest.
>
> Sam Peltzman, *Journal of Law and Economics* (August 1976), p. 212.

Two economic theories of regulation provide the basis for most of the analysis in the book: market failure and public choice. They are not in competition with each other. The market failure theory provides an economic rationale for what regulation ought to do—improve economic efficiency by correcting market failures—while the public choice theory provides an economic rationale for understanding why regulatory agencies and programs often do not deal effectively with the economic problem of inefficient allocation of resources. In observing the cases of market failure, proponents of the public choice theory seek to understand why regulators, even those mandated to correct allocational inefficiencies, appear to serve many masters—not just the consumer or public—usually in a manner that from a management perspective appears cumbersome, costly, inflexible, wasteful, and misdirected.

The market failure theory is rooted firmly in economics, particularly in that branch known as welfare economics. The public choice theory has in addition to an economic basis elements that stem from other disciplines—in particular history, political science, and law. Questions about government regulation that have been the concern of historians, political scientists, or legal scholars have only recently stimulated economists. These economists interested in achieving economic efficiency as the goal of regulation are at the same time taking the perspective of historians, looking at the effects of regulation, for example, as in the area of transportation where the responsive attitude toward the needs of the regulated industries has given rise to the capture theory of regulation.[1] The political scientists' and legal scholars' viewpoints have led regulators to pose questions relating to due process, legitimacy, and regulatory reform.[2] In that recent developments in the economic theory of regulation borrow from all these disciplines, they bring to center stage the behavior of regulators in responding to interest groups, and the processes by which regulatory programs are introduced, modified, and administered.

2.1   Market Failure Theory of Regulation

Market failure occurs when the free market produces too much or too little of some product or service and at too high or too low a price. The norm against which market failures are gauged of course is the amount and price of the product or service that would occur in a fully competitive market.[3] One frequently cited example of such a market failure or deviation from competition occurs when there are large economies of scale in a production process, as in some parts of the utility industry. This may result in the emergence of a single supplier who as a monopolist would have the profit incentive and the ability to produce too little and charge too much for their product.

A second familiar example of market failure relates to pollution. The market failure here is that one set of valuable inputs to a production process, including clean air and water, are priced too low to the producer. This results from our common ownership of these resources, which means that in a free market we are not fully compensated for their use. Public interest here requires that a market value be placed on these inputs and users be required to pay the price. If successful, pollution regulation would raise prices and lower output in the polluting industries and of course result in less pollution.

The list of market failures is not exhausted by natural monopoly and pollution, but these economic arguments have been most extensively used to justify regulatory programs, define their goals, and assess the cost effectiveness of regulations. Other regulatory programs have expounded the subject of safety, that the free market frequently does not yield the right amount of safety, so products and processes must be regulated to make them safer.[4]

In the financial industries many regulatory programs are based in part on the argument that the free market yields too much fraud manipulation and deception. The SEC as well as many federal and state banking regulations are primarily directed at reducing the amount of fraud or deception in financial transactions. Another market failure occurring in the financial industries is even more fundamental since it raises the spector of the competitive process itself being unstable and leading to destructive competition. Banking regulations that fix maximum interest rates that banks can pay, for example, have been justified on the basis of preventing the banking system from competitively destroying itself.

Market failure theory provides a basis for establishing a regulatory system in the public interest. It defines the most desirable state for securing the public interest as fully competitive prices and outputs; it provides means for assessing when market outcomes deviate substantially from competitive norms; it provides a set of regulatory goals against which the success of the regulatory program can be gauged; and it can provide for an ongoing assessment of the costs and effectiveness of the regulatory program.

The SEC, in order to conform to the tenets of market failure theory, would have been founded and continued for these fifty years (1) only after convincing evidence was available that price manipulation, fraud, and deceit were excessive, (2) only if regulatory programs could be designed and administered that would actually reduce these undesirable activities, and (3) only if the regulatory programs were not excessively costly compared to the value to society of reducing these activities.[5] During the Senate hearings of 1932 to 1934 that led to the securities acts, some unscrupulous people were exposed, but the evidence that they were able to manipulate stock prices is less than convincing.[6] In fact no documentation by the SEC is available that shows that their regulatory programs have reduced the amount of price manipulation fraud and deceit.[7] That these practices still exist is demonstrated by major public cases, such as Equity Funding, but we have no evidence that they are more or less prevalent than in pre-SEC days. Only one serious attempt has been made by the SEC to measure a major part of the social costs of its programs, but no ongoing program exists to measure systematically these costs and to use them in the decision-making process.

In failing to meet the criteria for successful regulation laid out by the market failure theory the SEC is hardly unique. Nearly all regulatory programs have fallen far short of dealing successfully with a real market failure in a cost effective manner. This universally negative finding about the ability to achieve economic efficiency through regulatory programs has led to two schools of thought. One abandons the notion that correcting market failures is a serious goal of regulatory agencies and instead views these agencies as an integral part of the political-economic system that has as a major function the reallocation of wealth among competing groups. In this view regulatory agencies serve the same function as legislators in imposing taxes on some groups and dispensing benefits to others, and they are subject to the same political pressures as legislators.

The other school of thought suggests that the failures of our regulatory agencies are due primarily to legal and procedural problems that can be corrected by certain reforms. A study by Roger Noll has summarized this view: ". . . nearly all regulation authorities, however structured and wherever lodged, are subject to generally similar criticisms: that their procedures are cumbersome, that they do not make their policies sufficiently clear, and that they tend to be overly responsive to the interests of the industries they regulate."[8]

A government-sponsored study of regulatory agencies, headed by Roy L. Ash, diagnosed the regulatory problem as one of inflexibility.[9] The procedures of the independent agencies, their commissioner structure, and most important their alleged independence of the president and Congress combine to make regulation cumbersome, slow, and inflexible. The Ash commission recommended four reforms:

1. Merge the three principal transportation agencies, the Interstate Commerce Commission, the Civil Aeronautics Board, and the Federal Maritime Commission, into a single transportation regulatory agency.

2. Divide the Federal Trade Commission into two agencies, a Federal Trade Practices Agency to deal with consumer protection and a Federal Antitrust Board to assume the FTC's responsibilities in antitrust enforcement.

3. Transfer promotional responsibilities from regulatory agencies to an appropriate executive department, specifically the CAB's program of subsidies for local service airlines to the Department of Transportation.

4. Transfer administration of the Public Utility Holding Company Act from the SEC to the Federal Power Agency.

These reforms may make the regulatory agencies more responsive to the president's wishes, but whether they would improve the performance of the agencies in promoting economic efficiency is much less certain.

Noll, Richard Schmalensee, and other students of the regulatory process have noted that legislation creating regulatory programs gives too much latitude to regulators and thereby make them too susceptible to political and economic pressures from Congress and from other interest groups, most notably the regulated industry. Schmalensee suggests making economic efficiency the single goal of legislation enabling regulation of the utility industry.[10]

Homer Kripke in his study of the SEC's corporate disclosure program also stresses the point that the large and growing program still has no clear goal after fifty years, thus no clear way to assess its effectiveness or the desirability of changes in the program.[11]

Reform-minded students of the regulatory process suggest that better legislation aimed at defining the goals of regulatory programs would improve performance. Focused regulatory programs would insulate regulators from special interest groups. Goals more precise than "protecting the public interest" would permit an assessment of the effectiveness of regulatory programs and make regulators accountable, as they clearly are not under present laws.

While it is possible to conceive of better regulatory laws and better administration of regulatory programs that deal with real market failures in a cost effective manner, the widespread absence of such laws and programs leaves a nagging suspicion that something more fundamental is amiss. It is this observation that is mainly responsible for some recent revisions in the economic theory of regulation that have placed more emphasis on the effect that regulation has on resource allocations and the process by which the public chooses which regulatory programs it wants.

2.2   Public Choice Theory of Regulation

Market failure theory fails to capture adequately the way in which regulation actually works in the real world. Recent developments in the economic theory of regulation, which for convenience we will refer to as public choice theory, attempt to fill this void. The theory is based on the fact that every regulation reallocates resources and in the process makes some groups or individuals (the recipients) richer and others (the regulatory taxpayers) poorer. Naturally any proposed regulation will attract the attention of both the beneficiaries and the payers, and they will express their support or opposition through political and economic channels.

The public choice theory of regulation views the birth and evolution of regulatory programs as a process in which individuals and groups express their preferences in a political-economic marketplace.[12] How individuals will respond to some regulatory proposal depends foremost on how the new regulation would affect their wealth. For example, if the regulation involves a large tax or subsidy for a number of people, then there may be a strong incentive for them to organize and oppose or support the regulation. Individuals that have a smaller economic stake in the regulation by comparison would have less incentive to participate in this political-economic market process.

Once individuals have established that they have a large stake in the proposed regulation, they must organize themselves effectively to bid for or against the regulation. The public choice theory identifies this as a crucial stage because the costs of organizing groups varies with their size; as the size of a group increases, the costs per member of effectively organizing rises too. The larger the group, beyond some point the larger the costs per member of organizing and therefore the less likely is the group to be effectively organized.

Groups that have a large stake in a regulation for which the costs of organizing are not excessive must then approach the law maker or regulator in the political-economic marketplace and indicate the strength of their support or opposition to the regulation. Although the theory subsumes all manner of support or opposition under the heading of votes, only the human imagination limits the ways in which support or opposition to the regulation can be delivered to the auctioneer.

The public choice theory has a number of important implications for the regulatory process, most important of which is that the public interest, as defined by the market failure theory, may not be an important consideration in the regulatory process. The success of a regulatory program hinges on the balancing of interests of effectively organized groups. Regulations are introduced, expanded, contracted, and eliminated in response to the groups' ability to organize effectively and bid for or against the regulation. Only by accident would this process lead to regulatory programs in the public interest; they are far more likely to be to the benefit of the small group—not the public interest.

Public choice theory suggests that regulations will tend to favor (subsidize) relatively small and well-organized groups that have a high per capita stake in the regulations, at the expense of relatively large, poorly organized groups with a lower per capita stake in the program. This pattern seems to hold in the SEC's major regulatory program, which requires about 10,000 corporations to prepare various forms periodically and when new capital is raised. The major supporters of these programs outside the SEC itself are securities lawyers, financial accountants, and others who earn their livelihood preparing the documents, and financial analysts, portfolio managers, and other securities market professionals who obtain the fruits of these labors at very little cost. The costs are borne by registered corporations who in turn pass them on to their customers, workers, owners, and suppliers in some unknown mix.

Corporate disclosure regulatory programs may also serve the public interest if they provide information that improves the pricing of securities and in that process reduces price manipulation, fraud, and deceit. These remain the major articulated reasons for the corporate disclosure program. Yet the evidence examined in chapter 3 suggests that corporate disclosure programs have had little success in achieving these goals. We estimate that they have succeeded in redirecting resources of over $1 billion per year, apparently from the public by small per capita amounts to several relatively small groups in large per capita amounts.

Another but now defunct SEC regulatory program of enforcing and setting fixed brokerage commission rates seems also to fit this general pattern. Fixed commissions were set generally above competitive rates and hence tended to transfer resources from investors to the securities industry. Investor groups, at least until about the mid-1960s, contained many members with a relatively small stake, while the benefited groups in the securities industry contained relatively few members with a higher per capita stake in the program.

The public choice theory also suggests that there may be many groups with different effective interests involved in the regulatory process and that the resulting regulatory program may tax or subsidize different groups at different rates, including exemptions or zero tax rates. The regulatory tax rate implicit in the corporate disclosure programs, for example, taxes small firms at a much higher rate per dollar of assets than larger firms. Special exemption and less costly reporting schemes have been experimented with by the SEC to deal with the special problems of small or new firms.

A more dramatic example of changing interests among the various groups participating in the regulatory process occurred in the fixed commission regulatory program during the 1960s. Institutional investors grew rapidly in importance during that period. Since fixed commission rates taxed large transactions much more heavily than small ones, the transfer of wealth implicit in fixed commissions was increasingly at the expense of that group. The regulatory structure adjusted at the beginning by setting lower rates for larger transactions, but the program was eventually abandoned. The SEC regulatory reform initiatives in market structure and exchange reorganization have not met with much success due to the opposition of the powerful and well-organized exchanges. Their per capita stake in the status quo and the dispersed interests of the taxed group—investors—has rendered the SEC's efforts to shape a national market system ineffective. Technological advances, which would have occurred without the interference of the SEC, have been the driving force in the national market system.

2.3   Comparison of the Two Theories

We are left then with two quite different economic theories of regulation. Market failure identifies various failures or deviations from the fully competitive marketplace and sets goals for regulatory programs that approximate free market solutions. Public choice utilizes an extended notion of market behavior as it expresses itself through the political system. Groups organize and express their support or opposition to regulatory programs, depending on the effects that the regulation will have on the wealth position of individuals in the group. The resulting regulatory structure may appear totally irrational from the market failure theory point of view and reflect instead the different and changing economic interests of competing groups in the economy.

There are also major differences between the theories in terms of how regulatory programs are managed. If the public interest criteria were the major driving force for regulatory programs, we would expect to find (1) clearly stated goals of the programs based on approximating the competitive outcome for prices and output, (2) substantial regulatory resources devoted to assessing the effectiveness of the stated goals, measuring both the costs and the benefits of the regulatory programs, and (3) policy discussions dominated by or at least substantially affected by these considerations. Managers of these regulatory programs would be rewarded for attaining regulatory goals in the least costly manner and for avoiding and eliminating excessively costly programs.

Public choice theory suggests that regulatory managers operate under a very different set of incentives to transfer resources from some groups, in such a manner as to minimize opposition to the regulatory tax to other groups that generate the most support for the program or agency. There is a disincentive for regulatory managers to discuss specific, measurable goals of the regulatory programs, to measure the size and direction of the wealth transfer involved, or to favor low-cost options when regulations are expanded. There is also a management incentive to make the regulatory process obscure and complicated and to impose high costs on those who would challenge regulatory decisions. Among other things this would help enforce the delicate balances struck among competing interest groups in the regulatory process.

Both the market failure and public choice theories are important in understanding an agency like the SEC. Even if all the SEC regulatory programs were to conform to the public choice model, for example, it is still interesting to ask whether a particular program such as corporate disclosure is in the public interest in the sense that it advances economic efficiency. The competitive economic model, and hence public interest criteria, should be the yardstick against which regulatory agencies and programs are measured.

Chapter 3

Corporate Disclosure

The Committee has concluded that, notwithstanding, the arguments of economists and others that the efficient market hypothesis, the random walk theory, and the strength of market forces have rendered obsolete or unnecessary much or all of the mandatory disclosure system administered by the Securities and Exchange Commission, these arguments are not sufficiently compelling to justify dismantling the existing system at this time.

Advisory Committee on Corporate Disclosure to the Securities and Exchange Commission (1978)

The disclosure system was founded, without investigations or serious consideration, on erroneous premises, namely, that the written SEC documents would be the primary, if not the only source, of investor information, that they would be used and understood by lay investors, and that they would be sufficient and adequate for that purpose.

Homer Kripke, *The SEC and Corporate Disclosure: Regulation in Search of a Purpose* (1979)

Over the years the SEC has become known with some justification as a disclosure agency. The corporate disclosure requirements for issuers of public securities are based on the notion that if investors are informed about the issues they can make proper investment decisions. This disclosure system was established by the Securities Act of 1933, the first of the New Deal securities regulation, because it was said to be in the public interest.

Certainly there are major benefits to society of having an SEC relate to the elaborate corporate disclosure system. But the disclosure system is also a major source of the SEC's social costs, directly through the costs of administering and expanding the system and indirectly through the costs imposed on the private sector in preparing the disclosure documents. In general regulators and others directly involved in regulatory programs have little incentive to document benefits or tally up social costs, so they rarely do this. Nonetheless, a literature addressing benefits and costs of the corporate disclosure system has begun to develop and provides the substance for our assessment of this SEC regulatory program. Is this SEC program in the public interest, or for that matter has it ever been in the public interest?

The SEC disclosure system requires certain periodic reports from registered corporations (forms 10-K, 10-Q, and 8-K) and certain reports registering newly issued securities (mainly S-1, S-7, S-14, and S-16).[1] In 1975, 54,640 periodic disclosure reports were filed by approximately 10,000 corporations, and 2,813 new issue registration documents were accepted by the SEC.

The number of companies reporting, and the types of reports required, have grown substantially since the enabling legislation was passed in the early 1930s, and this expansion of the corporate disclosure system appears to be accelerating. Some examples of this expansion include disclosure by bank-holding companies, disclosure of management perks, overseas payments, replacement cost accounting, and segmental or line-of-business accounting.

Like most regulatory programs the corporate disclosure system was designed to remedy a perceived market failure. In this case the market failure involved an allegedly fragile capital market where securities prices were said to be inefficient (not reflecting available information) and price manipulation was considered to be rife. The main rationale for corporate disclosure was that better information about the corporation should be required which would in turn enhance the pricing mechanisms through the buying and selling activities of better informed investors. If investors know more of the truth about the corporation, they will be able to make more intelligent investment decisions, and through this market activity the stock would be fairly priced. With capital markets fairer to the typical investor, the task of price manipulators would be more difficult.

As in many regulatory programs the mandatory corporate disclosure program has expanded over the years, with little attention paid to whether the intended benefits were achieved or any undesirable side effects emerged. The investigation of various parts of these questions (sometimes only addressing limited parts of the disclosure system) has been carried out for the most part by academicians.

Although the effects of corporate disclosure generally have been studied in the private sector, a recent government-sponsored study provides an interesting exception to this generalization. The exception is the study by the advisory committee to the SEC on corporate disclosure. This study addresses the questions of how corporate disclosure is used and provides for the first time high-quality estimates of some of the costs of the corporate disclosure program.

3.1   Pricing Efficiency and Corporate Disclosure

The corporate disclosure system relies heavily upon market efficiency—the ability of the market to reflect all available information through the pricing system. The theory of efficient pricing in asset markets has developed rapidly in recent years. Basically the theory posits that a market is efficient if asset prices reflect at each moment all information available. This hypothesis has been tested in many variants and in many different asset markets, usually in the form of statistical tests that relate current available information to future price movements or rates of return. If available information is useful in predicting future prices or returns, then there exists an opportunity to make abnormal profits by acting (buying or selling) on that information. If the current asset price does not fully reflect the available information, the market is said to be inefficient in pricing.

A major branch of the efficient market literature addresses the important question of what information is available. Information is not free and must be produced. In the securities markets information at the firm and industry levels is produced and disseminated by a small army of professionals, including over 14,000 securities analysts and many accountants and securities lawyers qualified to practice before the SEC.

In the absence of SEC-mandated corporate disclosure, the human and other resources involved in preparing and filing disclosures would be governed by the same economic principles that determine resource allocations elsewhere in a competitive market economy. Resources would flow into this activity until the addition of more resources would yield only a normal return. When the SEC requires more disclosure than would be forthcoming in the free market, additional resources are induced to engage in corporate information production. Indeed the basic economic question relating to corporate disclosure is whether the social benefits that these additional resources generate justify their social cost.[2]

Most studies of market efficiency test whether asset pricing reflects some part of the information produced in the disclosure process. These tests strongly support the notion that asset markets are efficient with respect to this information.[3]

During the senate hearings that led to the securities acts, asset markets were generally portrayed as fickle, spurious, easily manipulated, and therefore inefficient. William A. Gray, council for the Senate Committee on Banking and Currency during the stock exchange practice hearing, described the securities markets as follows: "Evidence will be found in the record that will leave no doubt in the minds of the committee that powerful interests, operating on a large scale in a particular stock can so manipulate the market and control the price of that stock in normal times as to accomplish almost any desired result." [4]

If this view were correct, then investors entering the market could not be confident that securities prices reflected available information. Rather investors would be at the mercy of manipulators who could set the price anywhere they wanted. This view of the securities markets as extremely fragile, susceptible to price manipulation, inefficient, and hence unfair prevailed and was a major if not the major justification for establishing the SEC.

The SEC's primary attempt to strengthen the market and protect investors from unfair, manipulated prices was in establishing the corporate disclosure system. More and better information for investors was seen as a way to improve the pricing mechanism and make price manipulation more difficult. One of the more sophisticated observers of the period, the future Justice William O. Douglas, explained how the corporate disclosure system, working through the professional information producers, would lead to a stronger or more efficient asset-pricing market: "Even though an investor has neither the time, money, or intelligence to assimilate the mass of information in the registration statement, there will be those who can and who will do so whenever there is a broad market. The judgment of those experts will be reflected in the market price." [5]

As the disclosure system expanded since 1934, the regulatory program has become ever more directed toward providing for a better informed investing public. In a recent report the SEC Advisory Committee on Corporate Disclosure described the intent of corporate disclosure as follows: "To assure the public availability in an efficient and reasonable manner on a timely basis of reliable, firm-oriented information material to informed investment, and corporate suffrage decision making." [6]

The logic of the SEC's position that more public information leads to better investment decisions, hence to a better pricing mechanism for assets, seems unassailable. Yet the important factual questions remain as to whether the pricing mechanisms actually improved as a result of corporate disclosure and, if so, whether they improved enough to justify the added costs of mandated disclosure. If they did in fact improve, then investors benefited by trading in markets where prices reflect a broader or more accurate set of information and where stock price manipulators face a more difficult task in pushing prices away from equilibrium.

In recent years several studies have been made to determine how the corporate disclosure system has affected the pricing of securities. These studies utilize the market model that relates the rate of return on an individual stock to the rate of return on a diversified portfolio of stocks, as shown in equation (3.1):

$$r_i = \hat{\alpha} + \hat{\beta} r_M + \hat{e}, \tag{3.1}$$

where

r_i = the rate of return on the stock of company i,

r_M = the rate of return on a diversified portfolio of stocks,

$\hat{\alpha}$ = a statistical estimate of the intercept of the line describing the relation between r_i and r_M,

$\hat{\beta}$ = a statistical estimate of the slope of the line describing the relationship between r_i and r_M,

$\hat{e}$ = the error of the regression, assumed to be normally distributed with zero mean, and also the return on the stock of company i not explained by the market.

The market model has been used to study the effects of corporate disclosure by estimating equation (3.1) over two time periods, one prior to and one following the imposition of required corporate disclosure. If corporate disclosure improves the pricing mechanism, that improvement should be reflected either in a change in $\hat{\beta}$ (the beta) or in the distribution (variance) of $\hat{e}$. Both of these changes reflect altered risk: a changed beta implies altered market evaluation of systematic risk, and a change in the variance of the residuals implies changed unsystematic or firm-related risk. For example, if the market reassessed the relationship of the return on an individual stock with and without corporate disclosure, there would be a significant difference in $\hat{\beta}$ after SEC corporate disclosure. A second test relates to the unexplained or residual return $\hat{e}$. If better information leads to more accurate pricing, then the variance of $\hat{e}$ would change and presumably become smaller.[7]

George J. Benston measures the costs and benefits of mandated disclosure, using a number of hypotheses relating to the success of the periodic disclosure requirements of the Securities Exchange Act of 1934.[8] Briefly the 1934 act requires that corporations issuing registered and/or traded stock on a securities exchange file with the SEC detailed financial statements and supporting information (form 10-K) within four months of the close of the fiscal year. In addition the same corporations must file other periodic (form 10-Q) and nonperiodic current reports (form 8-K) whenever substantial changes in earnings, management, asset valuation or legal states occur. As Benston points out, mandatory disclosure was chosen as an alternative to the SEC's approving or disapproving securities for acceptable exchange trading to (1) assure the fair and efficient operation of capital markets, (2) prevent fraud and manipulation, and (3) provide shareholders with equal access to adequate and relevant information about investment decisions.

Benston uses the market model to test whether the published financial data required by the SEC's mandatory disclosure requirements contain economic information as measured by shareholder returns. Altogether the shareholder returns of 466 NYSE companies were examined in pre-SEC and post-SEC periods. Of these companies 296 voluntarily disclosed sales information before the establishment of the SEC. The calculated statistics from the market model from each of the two periods for Benston's analysis include the beta, the regression residuals, and the variance of those residuals. The betas of the non-disclosure group changed less when the corporations were forced to disclose their sales in the post-SEC period than did the betas of the disclosure group, which is inconsistent with the notion of the SEC's reducing risk by mandating disclosure. The pattern of average residuals for both groups of stocks is similar: the variance of the residuals is lower between February 1934, when hearings on the 1934 act began, and June 1934, when the act became law, as compared to preceding and subsequent periods. Finally the variance of the residuals for the disclosure group was actually higher than that of the nondisclosure group, implying that the latter group was less risky. The change in residual variance over the period examined for each stock group was about the same, however. Benston concludes that the evidence is only consistent with the hypothesis "that the disclosure provisions of the '34 act were of no apparent value to investors." [9]

To determine whether SEC mandatory disclosure has reduced shareholder losses, Benston examines the proportion of both disclosure and nondisclosure firms that either merged or delisted. These two events were assumed to produce more than normal losses for stockholders. But a lower proportion of the nondisclosure group merged or delisted than of the disclosure group, implying again that the latter group is somewhat more risky. Disclosure then does not seem to reduce losses or shareholder risk. Rather, based on the net new issues of securities relative to assets and private placements, the 1934 act "may have reduced the value of stock markets to corporations and therefore to investors." [10]

Since the analysis of the residuals indicated that the 1934 act had no differential effect on disclosure and nondisclosure companies, and since there is considerable evidence that markets have been efficient in the post-SEC period, Benston concludes that "the market was efficient before the legislation was enacted, at least with respect to the financial data." [11] Moreover, runs tests confirmed the random walk hypothesis in the pre-SEC period; the SEC did not create a fairer game for investors. In Benston's words, "the disclosure requirements of the Securities Exchange Act of 1934 had no measurable positive effect on the securities traded on the NYSE. There appears to have been little basis for the legislation and no evidence that it was needed or desirable. Certainly there is doubt that more disclosure is warranted." [12]

To examine whether the SEC has been successful at preventing fraud and manipulation, Benston examined the voluntary disclosure practices of corporations whose stock prices were alleged to have been manipulated by groups or pools of investors prior to the establishment of the SEC and compared their disclosure practices to the practices of all NYSE-listed companies. Since there was no significant difference in accounting procedures between the two groups, Benston concludes that the operations of these pools "owed little to the non-disclosure of accounting data." [13]

The related hypothesis that investors in newly issued securities fared worse in pre-SEC days than in post-SEC days was first examined by George Stigler in 1964. He compared the performance of eighty common stock issues by corporations formed in the period 1923 to

1928 for the first five years after issue with forty-seven similar new issues between 1947 and 1955. In both periods the performance of the new issue prices was adjusted for movements in the market. He performed a similar comparison for newly issued preferred stock. Stigler concludes from his study that "the SEC registration requirement had no important effect on the quality of new securities sold to the public."[14]

In a critical reply to this study Irwin Friend and Edward S. Herman showed that Stigler's and their evidence was consistent with a somewhat better performance relative to the market for new issues in the post-SEC period.[15] They conclude that post-SEC investors in new issues were statistically significantly better off in at least some years after their initial investment and in no case worse off than investors prior to the SEC.

The Stigler paper and the Friend-Herman critical reply touched off a series of caustic exchanges in the academic journals and in governmental and regulatory circles.[16] As a result Stigler corrected a number of the errors in the disclosure tests presented in his article and suggested that some of these tests may even have been inappropriately severe and presented revised data. Nevertheless, Stigler maintained his earlier conclusion, "that the SEC review procedures had not significantly improved the market performance of new issues relative to outstanding issues. The data revisions and the new analysis do not call for amendment to this conclusion."[17] But Friend and Herman still questioned Stigler's interpretation of the data, pointing to a cumulative weight of evidence (although not statistically significant) that favored the hypothesis that the influence of the SEC on newly issued security returns has been positive.

The second testable proposition relating to the manner in which the registration disclosure may have helped investors concerns the variance of returns on new issues. Whether or not mandated disclosure removes a bias toward overpricing new issues, it may reduce the variance of returns on new issues. If the reduction uniformly affects all securities, this alleged benefit is of no value to investors because very high and very low returns are equally reduced, leaving investors as a group no better or worse off. Moreover diversified portfolios of new issues could have identical risk/return properties in either the high or low variance case. Owners of undiversified portfolios of new issues would be better off, however, in the low variance case if they have an aversion toward risk.

Here the evidence presented is unambiguous: standard deviations of return were much larger for new issues in the pre-SEC period. The difference is overstated in the sense that the overall variability of the stock market was greater in the 1920s than in the early 1950s, but the difference would remain even if this adjustment were made.[18]

Benston also studied the question of whether or not the SEC improved the new issues market but from a slightly different viewpoint.[19] First, to determine whether the new issue stock market was improved in relation to capital spending, Benston examined new security issues (net of redemptions) as a percent of gross expenditures on plant and equipment and then as a percent of expenditures on new capital expansion (net of replacement expenditures). These calculations were made from business cycle trough to trough for the pre- and post-SEC periods to control for business trends in the two periods. Further, even when adjustments are made for the bias against stock as a result of the differential dividend and capital gains tax treatment, which would be expected to bias stock issues in the post-SEC period document, Benston finds that "the SEC had a somewhat perverse effect on the use of securities markets for new financing by corporations, if all other factors really are equal. When a subjective adjustment for the income tax effects is made, the difference between the pre- and post-SEC periods probably is not significant. Hence it appears that the SEC has not had a positive effect on the use of stock markets by corporations."[20]

In a second, although reportedly suggestive, empirical test Benston hypothesized that the industries likely to be subject to the most bias in their accounting statements, as a result of the conservative reporting requirements of the SEC, would be the most likely to utilize private placements as a means of escaping SEC registration. Although data were only available from 1953 to 1966 (and thus a pre- and post-test was not possible), those industries thought to be subject to the most accounting bias were found to use more private placements than those industries whose assets could be accurately portrayed by the conservative SEC reporting bias.[21] It should be noted that no control was available for the pre-SEC period to determine whether the rankings compiled in the post-SEC periods were continued into the post-SEC period.

To return to our original question, has the development of the mandatory corporate disclosure system improved pricing efficiency in the asset markets? The evidence reviewed here provides no support for this notion, as it relates to markets for secondary issues, and at best weak or inconclusive support, as it relates to markets for new issues. It would seem that, if we are to discover the benefits of the SEC corporate disclosure system, we must look elsewhere.

3.2   Equal Access to Corporate Information and Corporate Disclosure

During the investigation of the early 1930s trading on new information by corporate officers and other insiders was also viewed as a form of unfairness in the market. From an economic perspective this so-called insider trading was different from the price manipulative practices believed possible through pooling operations. Indeed the two alleged abuses produce opposite market impacts. Stock price manipulation moves a price away from its equilibrium or efficiently priced level, and insider trading, reflecting new information, moves the stock price toward a new equilibrium. Thus insider trading serves the useful economic function of moving stock prices to a new equilibrium.[22]

The corporate disclosure system was seen by some as a method of providing equal access to information, thus alleviating some of the perceived unfairness. In fact the long time lag between preparation and public availability in corporate disclosure documents, as well as other problems with their style and length, apparently make them of little direct use to public investors. This suspicion was confirmed in the study by the SEC Advisory Committee on Corporate Disclosure.

The committee report noted that SEC mandatory disclosure forms are far too lengthy (in some cases up to several hundred pages) and technical in nature, requiring considerable documentation of the accounting methods used in the preparation of the financial statements filed with the SEC and sent to the shareholders as part of the annual statement. Moreover, because some of the descriptive parts of the mandatory documents repeat the prior year's accounting methods and changes in methods, it is sometimes difficult to understand the forms without simultaneously reading those from the year before. The SEC filings in fact rarely are used directly by investors to make investment decisions. As part of its study of the disclosure system the committee surveyed a large sample of public investors and asked, among other things, what major sources of information investors relied upon. The survey revealed that investors relied upon three major sources for useful information: stockbrokers, company annual reports, and daily newspapers, with the annual report being the most common source.[23]

The SEC filings never showed up as a primary or secondary reference for such items as financial statements, security prices, earnings, sales and products.[24] Further the companies surveyed reported that on average, less than 1 percent of all shareowners requested the 10-K report for each of the years 1974 and 1975.[25] Similar results were reported by brokerage house registered representatives regarding requests from customers for SEC-filed documents.[26]

Based on other results of the advisory committee's findings, the SEC mandatory filings appear to be more important to security analysts than to any other group of participants in the disclosure process: 77.8 percent of the sell-side respondents (those who sell research to brokerage house customers) and 91.3 percent of the buy-side respondents (purchasers of research such as mutual funds, pension funds, and banks) reported that form 10-K was vital to them.[27] Other mandatory SEC reports were not so often reported to be vital. On a substantive item basis such as product lines, sales, and corporate organization SEC filings were cited as a source of information by security analysts, but the importance of the SEC reports varied considerably across different financial items.[28]

In sum the SEC filings appear to be little used directly by investors but are widely used by market processors of information, as was anticipated by Justice Douglas.

3.3   The Relationship between Owners and Managers and Corporate Disclosure

Some view the capital market as unfair in yet another sense. This view stems from the divergence of interests between investors, whose primary motivation is to achieve the highest rate of return on invested funds for a given level of risk, and corporate managers, whose self-interest will sometimes be in conflict with this goal.

Prior to the establishment of the SEC, as well as more recently, the private market has generated a number of mechanisms to deal with this inherent conflict. These have taken the form of various contractual restrictions on the decision-making latitude of managers, as well as the presence of boards of directors to oversee the managers' actions and protect the interests of owners and others. An additional common arrangement was an agreement between owners and managers that required periodic detailed reporting on the performance of the corporation, which among other things provided a systematic monitoring of the effects of decisions made by management. The extent to which an unregulated market would engage in these disclosures or monitor contracts has been documented by Benston, who reports that before the 1933 and 1934 acts all the NYSE-listed corporations "published financial statements: most were audited by CPAs and about two-thirds gave shareholders such detailed data as sales (turnover), depreciation and cost of goods sold. In the U.K. most companies report more data than are required by law. Publications of much financial data by a large proportion of publicly owned corporations then does not appear to be due primarily to government requirements."[29]

The nature of contracts between owners and managers that serve a monitoring function through public disclosure by managers has received attention from economists only in recent years.[30] An important theoretical framework for evaluating these monitoring programs, and their effects on owners and managers, has recently been developed by Jensen and Meckling.[31] We can use this theory to show the effects of these contracts in an unregulated market and then assess the effects of imposing corporate disclosure on top of the privately determined public disclosure. This exercise will be useful in identifying a major incentive for voluntary disclosure, and it will also reveal some differences in effects of voluntary as opposed to mandatory corporate disclosure.

Figure 3.1 shows how the different interests of owners and managers would be resolved in an efficient market, where the actions of managers are fully anticipated. We use a set of assumptions that restricts the problem to a sequence of identical periods without risk, government, sophisticated financial instruments, or monitoring costs.[32] The figure gives the relationship between the market value of an owner-managed firm and the market value of the stream of the manager's expenditures on nonpecuniary benefits.[33] $\overline{V}F$ describes the feasible trade-off between firm market value $\overline{V}$ and nonpecuniary expenditure F, the budget constraint. If the only argument in the owner-manager's utility function were pecuniary wealth V, then the decision made would be to maximize V at $\overline{V}$.

However, nonpecuniary benefits derived from capturing for personal use the inputs and activities of the firms also may yield utility to the owner-manager. As Jensen and Meckling note, utility to the owner-manager can be

. . . generated by various nonpecuniary aspects of his entrepreneurial activities such as the physical appointments of the

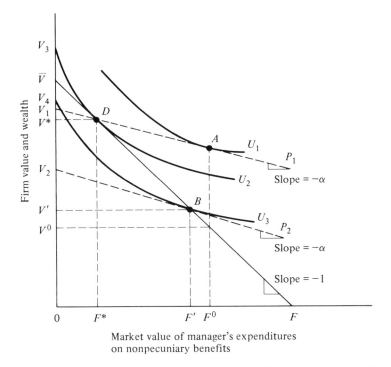

Figure 3.1 Value of the firm without agency costs (Source: Jenson and Meckling 1976, p. 316)

office, the attractiveness of the secretarial staff, the level of employee discipline, the kind and amount of charitable contributions, personal relations ("love," "respect," etc.) with employees, a larger than optimal computer to play with, purchase of production inputs from friends, etc. The optimum mix (in the absence of taxes) of the various pecuniary and nonpecuniary benefits is achieved when the marginal utility derived from an additional dollar of expenditure (measured net of any productive effects) is equal for each nonpecuniary item and equal to the marginal utility derived from an additional dollar of after tax purchasing power (wealth).[34]

   This subjective trade-off by the manager-owner between firm market value and nonpecuniary expenditures, under normal assumptions of positive and diminishing marginal utility, defines the indifference curves U_1, U_2, and U_3 in figure 3.1. Given these preferences, the utility-maximizing combination of expenditures on nonpecuniary benefits and of wealth is given by the tangency of U_2 and the budget constraint line $\overline{V}F$. In this case the equilibrium market value of the firm would be V^*, and the amount of nonpecuniary benefits consumed would be F^*.

If the owner-manager now sells a fraction $(1 - \alpha)$ of the firm to outside owners (nonvoting stock only to insure no control over the owner-manager), the incentive structure changes, since the owner-manager no longer bears the full cost, loss in wealth, of increasing expenditures on nonpecuniary benefits. The owner-manager will now correctly perceive the budget constraint represented by P_1 and therefore increase expenditures on nonpecuniary benefits out to F^0, leading to a value for the firm of only V^0. In this scenario the outside owners are fooled, paying $(1 - \alpha)V^*$ for the firm and seeing their wealth fall to $(1 - \alpha)V^0$ as the owner-manager adjusts upward the nonpecuniary benefits.

In the alternative case, when prspective outside owners can anticipate this behavior of the owner-manager, they will be willing to pay only the expected value of the firm. This forces the solution to point B which represents a firm value less than V^0 but still on the original budget constraint. Intuitively any tangency above the line $\overline{V}F$ would require outside owners to sustain a loss, and any tangency below the line P_1 would require the owner-manager to sustain a loss; thus V^1 is the fair price.[35]

The first main result then is that, if the behavior of owner-managers can be anticipated, outside owners will pay only a fair price for their portion of the firm. This occurs even though outside owners have absolutely no control over the manager, except their ability to buy and sell freely the nonvoting stock.

A possible further adjustment can occur through corporate disclosure and other monitoring expenditures to improve the manager's position without hurting the position of outside owners. The usual monitoring expenditures besides disclosure are auditing costs and insurance against the manager's malfeasance. If the manager's expenditures on nonpecuniary benefits decline, as the present value of monitoring expenses, M, increase, the expenditures would be borne by the manager. Since the owners are on the budget constraint, they have no incentive to pay through wealth losses. Managers, however, could gain by paying. The line $BCEG$ in figure 3.2 describes the feasible combinations of nonpecuniary benefits and market values of the firm for various levels of monitoring expenses M. Outside owners of course will be indifferent between buying part of the firm at a point like B, with no monitoring expenses, or at a point like D, with moni-

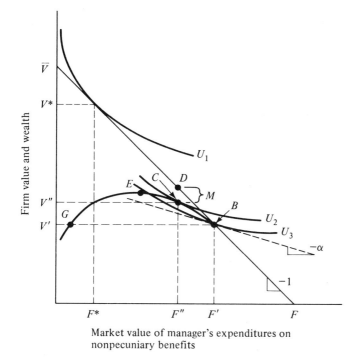

Figure 3.2 Value of the firm with agency costs (Source: Jenson and Meckling 1976, p. 324)

toring expenses equal to $\overline{DC}$; in both cases the price of the firm is fair. The manager will prefer the point C, which is on a higher indifference curve, illustrating the manager's preference for some disclosure.

This analysis shows that the manager in general has an incentive to create a contract that will monitor his behavior and thereby reduce his nonpecuniary benefits and increase his wealth. Further the assumption of efficient pricing of the firm assures that outside owners are indifferent to the amount of monitoring, so that the present value of the manager's nonpecuniary benefits and the monitoring costs are fully accounted for in price.

This theory can be extended to show some of the effects on managers and outside owners of a government-mandated monitoring or disclosure policy. As depicted in figure 3.2, a level of mandatory disclosure that requires less expenditure than $\overline{DC}$ would not affect the equilibrium point C, as long as the type of mandated disclosure information is identical to part of the disclosure that would occur in the free market. This describes the situation in the United Kingdom, where more than the required amount is freely disclosed.

Where mandated disclosure exceeds the amount that would be forthcoming in the free market, equilibrium will occur farther to the left, on the line segment $BCEG$. An interesting and counterintuitive result is that, if mandated disclosure is imposed (unexpectedly) on existing corporations, rather than newly formed corporations, the existing owners can enjoy a one-time wealth gain, a one-time wealth loss, or no change in wealth, depending on the portion of the line segment $BCEG$ to which the higher disclosure expenditures force the equilibrium. Thus, for example, the current drive to require disclosure of management perks may indeed hurt investors if the costs of supplying this information exceed the value of reduced perks because of fear of disclosure, and if investors are not now fooled systematically by the amount of perks. By comparison managers are made worse off in all cases of mandated disclosure because they are moved to a lower indifference curve.

Perhaps the most interesting result of this analysis is that, if owners correctly anticipate managers' behavior (if the pricing of securities accurately reflects managers' behavior), then mandatory disclosure will not in general help investors. But mandatory disclosure could benefit investors if it allowed them to anticipate better the behavior of managers. The importance of this conclusion is that it makes the benefits of mandatory disclosure depend on the effects that disclosure has on the pricing of securities. Any benefits to investors should be observable in an improved pricing mechanism.

3.4   Estimated Costs of SEC Corporate Disclosure

In each case of an alleged market failure examined in preceding sections, we conclude that the SEC disclosure system would benefit investors only if it improved the pricing mechanism for securities. Economic theory implies that insider trading would improve market efficiency. There is no empirical support for the notion that the SEC disclosure has improved the pricing mechanism for existing securities and only weak support for the notion that the SEC registration of newly issued securities has benefited investors. Yet the existence of the SEC disclosure system, however tenuous and modest its benefits are to investors, may be justified if the total costs to society of the program are sufficiently small.

A complete accounting of the costs of mandatory corporate disclosure includes all disclosure-related costs in excess of those that corporations would voluntarily have expended in an unregulated market (point *B* in figure 3.1). These costs include extra legal, accounting, auditing, and printing expenditures associated with the more detailed information in required documents. They can also include short-term fixed costs associated with more elaborate accounting and auditing systems and larger in-house legal departments than would be needed in the absence of mandated disclosure. A third category of costs involves regulatory delays and a general loss of management flexibility. A final cost that might be borne by individual companies, but not necessarily in full by society, would be any competitive disadvantage caused by an elaborate, mandated disclosure.

Until the recently published report of the Advisory Committee on Corporate Disclosure, no systematic attempt seems to have been made to measure any of these costs. The committee directed its staff to sample a small number of reporting companies to determine some of the costs associated with preparing the major disclosure forms for new securities (S-1, S-7, S-14, S-16) and also the general periodic disclosure forms (10-K, 8-K, 10-Q).

The cost information requested from issuers was restricted to fully variable costs. The surveyed firms were specifically instructed not to allocate to the preparation costs of documents any general overhead expenses. Nor were the firms to include any costs incurred initially to set up new or additional accounting or auditing systems to meet mandated disclosure standards. The only costs included then are those that could be immediately and fully eliminated if mandatory corporate disclosure were removed.

The quality of these data as a measure of fully variable costs of mandatory disclosure for the firms surveyed is probably very good. An elaborate questionnaire was followed up with interviews by well-trained staff who filled in any missing data. The sample was rather small—only 22 out of about 10,000 registered firms. Unfortunately little attempt was made to make the sample of firms representative of the population of reporting firms. As a result, while the quality of the data is high, the sample is not scientific.

3.5   Estimated Costs of Filing 10-K, 10-Q, and 8-K

In table 3.1 we combine the committee's sample results for variable costs of producing 10-K, 10-Q, and 8-K by firm size, with our estimates of the number of firms in each asset category. This yields an estimated annual cost of filing these documents in 1975 of $213 million.

Due to the smallness of the sample of firms the $213 million should be considered a ballpark estimate. In addition the estimate contains some known biases. Most important of these is that the survey questionnaire purposely excluded some costs associated with the SEC disclosure forms 10-K, 10-Q, and 8-K, which would not be borne by reporting firms if these forms were not required. The known bias would thus tend to understate costs of the periodic SEC disclosure by an unknown amount. The possible size of this bias will be explored when we discuss estimates of voluntary disclosure costs. A second bias arises because we have not included the SEC's costs in administering their periodic disclosure documents. The total SEC budget in 1975 was about $50 million, and no more than one-fourth of this, or $12.5 million, was devoted to administering periodic disclosure. To keep our cost estimate on the conservative side, we will ignore this component in the following discussions.

In determining the social desirability of this part of the SEC disclosure system, we need to weigh the $213 million of costs in 1975 against the social benefits of the program in that year. The evidence presented earlier on the effect of periodic disclosure on the pricing mechanism only addressed the problem of whether there were any benefits through improved pricing and not the more difficult question of placing a value on that improvement. Those results suggested that there were no pricing efficiency benefits, and thus, if there are no other social benefits to the program, the SEC disclosure system fails the cost-benefit test of social desirability: public interest is not well served.

However, some groups in society clearly benefit from this regulatory program: for example, those who enjoy increased demand for their services to produce the disclosures such as securities lawyers, financial accountants, auditors, and printers and those who receive the reports essentially without charge. Of the groups surveyed by the Advisory Committee on Corporate Disclosure most financial analysts viewed the reports as vital to their work, while other groups including investors found the reports of much less use. If analysts were able to improve the pricing mechanism by using the reports, then society

Table 3.1 Cost estimates of preparing 10-K, 10-Q, and 8-K corporate disclosure documents, by size of corporation, fiscal 1976

Assets	(1) 10-K filings ($1,000)	(2) Three 10-Q filings ($1,000)	(3) Two 8-K filings ($1,000)	(4) 10-K, 10-Q, and 8-K ($1,000)	(5) Number of firms[b]	(6) Total cost ($1 million)[c]
Over $1 billion	45.3 (8)[a]	11.2 (8)	.6 (6)	57.1	734	41.9
$100 million to $1 billion	13.3 (6)	5.6 (6)	.7 (6)	19.6	1,859	36.4
Less than $100 million	10.7 (7)	6.7 (8)	1.4 (9)	18.8	7,191	135.2
			Totals		9,784	213.5

Sources: Financial data from "Report of the Advisory Committee on Corporate Disclosure to the Securities and Exchange Commission," House Committee on Interstate and Foreign Commerce, Committee Print 95-29, November 3, 1977, p. 27.
[a]Number of observations.
[b]Estimate of number of reporting firms by asset size are based on a 2 percent sample taken from the *Directory of Companies Required to File Annual Reports with the Securities and Exchange Commission under the Securities Exchange Act of 1934*, dated June 30, 1976.
[c]The total cost is obtained by multiplying columns 4 and 5.

would benefit, and a case could be made for producing these reports at the expense of corporations who in turn pass the costs off to customers, suppliers, workers, management, debtors, and other investors. But if these reports do not improve the pricing mechanism, or have other social benefits, then those who use the reports should pay in full for them. In 1975, for example, some 14,000 financial analysts used these reports, with costs amounting to over $15,000 per analyst for the forms 10-K, 8-K, and 10-Q.

Notice that in table 3.1 periodic disclosure costs vary by firm size. Total variable costs shown in column 4 increase with firm size but not at the same rate as firm size. To some extent this reflects a bias in the survey. Large firms tend to do more of the report preparation with in-house resources and are not allowed to allocate all of those costs in the survey. Smaller firms, who tend to depend mostly on outside services, come closer to reporting full costs. Yet this regulatory tax appears to be hardest on smaller firms.

3.6   Estimated Costs of SEC New Issue Disclosure

The committee's cost sample also included twenty-two separate filings on the four registration documents S-1, S-7, S-14, and S-16. These forms must be filed with and approved by the SEC before corporations can issue new stock. We took a 10 percent sample of the SEC daily *News Digest,* which reports registration filings, and estimated that 1,482 of these documents were filed in 1975 by all registered firms. This leaves over 1,000 registration filings of S-8, for example, out of our cost estimates. Therefore in addition to the sample biases listed earlier an exclusion of about 40 percent of total filings would lead us to underestimate the full cost of the new issue disclosure system.

In table 3.2 we present cost estimates by firm size of filing the forms S-1, S-7, S-14, and S-16. The additional cost imposed by these four forms is $192 million for 1975. As before the estimate makes no allowance for the direct SEC costs of administering this program.

One way of gauging the significance of the $192 million is to compare it to the roughly $40 billion raised in 1975 by the firms included in our sample. New issue registration adds about .5 cent per dollar of capital raised to the cost of raising new capital. The proper comparison for this is what the .5 cent adds to the transactions cost of issuing new capital. For example, if 5 percent is an average cost of raising new

Table 3.2 Net cost estimates of preparing registration disclosure documents S-1, S-7, S-14, and S-16, by size of corporation, fiscal 1975

Asset size	S-1 ($1,000)	Number filed	S-7 ($1,000)	Number filed	S-14 ($1,000)	Number filed	S-16 ($1,000)	Number filed	Total cost ($1,000)
Over $1 billion	105.2	90	183.7	251	151.5	40	2.1	30	61,700
$100 million to $1 billion	49.8	140	122.8	241	204.5	40	2.1	110	44,800
Less than $100 million	123.6	331	163.4	20	257.5	160	2.1	30	85,400
Overall average	105.2	561	163.4	512	204.5	240	2.1	170	191,900

Sources: Financial data from "Report of the Advisory Committee on Corporate Disclosure," House Committee on Interstate and Foreign Commerce, Committee Print 95-29, November 3, 1977. Registrations filed were developed from a 1 in 10 sample of the registrations listed in the *SEC News Digest*, issues 75-1, dated January 2, 1975, through 75-250, dated December 30, 1975.

capital, these SEC regulations would account for about 10 percent of total transactions costs.

The estimated costs of registration per dollar of capital raised, while averaging .5 cent, varies greatly from form to form and also across firm size. The highest costs in this sample were for small firms filing S-1 documents, at a cost of 2.7 cents per dollar of capital raised. Lowest regulatory costs were for medium-sized firms filing the simpler S-16, at a cost of .03 cent per dollar of capital raised. One important economic question is whether this enormous variability in regulatory cost is matched by a similar range in regulatory benefits. To answer this question would require examining the market experience of firms filing each of the different forms. If there were little difference in market behavior, dramatic reductions in the costs of this regulatory program could be achieved by allowing most or all firms to shift from the more costly forms S-1, S-7, and S-14 to the least costly form S-16.

The samples underlying the cells in table 3.2 are too small to allow strong conclusions concerning the effect of firm size on costs of registration of new issues. One cell is based on a single observation. However, we should note that for each form where we have observations on smaller and larger firms, the costs per dollar of capital raised is higher for smaller firms. Medium-sized firms filing S-1 pay .09 cent per dollar of capital raised, while small firms, as noted earlier, pay 2.7 cents per dollar of capital raised. For S-7 large firms pay .3 cent per dollar of capital raised, while medium-sized firms pay .4 cent. Large firms filing S-14 pay .5 cent per dollar of capital raised, while small firms pay 4.2 cents.

In sum the four registration forms S-1, S-7, S-14, and S-16 imposed about $192 million of regulatory costs in 1975. A full accounting of the costs of the entire new issue regulatory program would show larger costs, perhaps by a substantial amount. The two major biases in the $192 million estimate would tend to understate true costs. First, approximately 40 percent of the filings are excluded from this cost estimate. Second, the committee's cost data tend to be conservative, since they exclude certain cost items related to mandatory disclosure. Costs of registration appear to vary greatly according to type of firm and its size, posing a greater burden to smaller firms. Overall the cost of filing the four corporate disclosure forms amounts to about .5 cent per dollar of capital raised in 1975.

3.7   A Comparison of Voluntary and SEC-Mandated Periodic Disclosure Costs

There are strong market incentives for corporations (management) to devote resources to disclosure and other monitoring programs, quite aside from the SEC regulatory programs. The committee's findings are shown in table 3.3, with voluntary disclosure costs about ten times larger than those related to mandatory disclosure.

However, the committee's cost sample is conservative. Some of the costs included in voluntary disclosure categories should instead be in mandatory disclosure categories. If the periodic mandatory disclosure system were terminated, firms would reduce costs by more than the $213 million estimate, because some overhead expenses would be curtailed as well as perhaps some internal legal and accounting expenses. Moreover, accounting and auditing expenditures might be reduced in the absence of SEC requirements. We have no basis for estimating how much of the voluntary expenses fall in these categories. But it may be worth noting that, if 10 percent of voluntary expenses are actually related to SEC requirements, then our cost estimates for forms 10-K, 10-Q, and 8-K would double to about $400 million for 1975.

As shown in table 3.3, the costs of voluntary and mandated periodic disclosure vary by firm size, with small firms devoting a much larger proportion of assets to these disclosures than large firms. In general both private and regulatory costs of capital are higher for small firms. Excluded from our sample are the very small firms whose costs may rise to prohibitive ranges.

In table 3.3 regulatory costs, as a percent of assets, rise much faster as firm size declines than do voluntary disclosure costs. This in fact does not reflect the real world pattern because large firms tend to understate regulatory costs more than small firms. Because large firms have ample in-house legal and accounting resources, they can underestimate regulatory costs more than smaller firms.

3.8   Summary

In the corporate disclosure system the benefits to investors have been expressed in different ways: to help investors make better informed decisions, to improve confidence in securities markets, to protect

Table 3.3 Costs of voluntary and mandatory periodic disclosure by corporations, as a percent of assets, 1975

Firm size (assets)	Number of firms	Voluntary disclosure				Mandatory periodic disclosure		
		Certified end of year statement ($1,000)	Annual report ($1,000)	Total cost ($1,000)	Cost as a percent of assets	Costs of 10K, 10Q, and 8K ($1,000)	Total cost ($1,000)	Cost as a percent of assets
Large ($2.6 billion)	734	728.4	149.9	644,700	0.034	57.1	41,900	0.0022
Medium ($268 million)	1,859	243.2	194.7	814,100	0.163	19.6	36,400	0.0073
Small ($26 million)	7,191	72.9	47.3	864,400	0.462	18.8	135,200	0.0723
Total	9,784			2,323,200			213,500	

Sources: Financial data from "Report of the Advisory Committee on Corporate Disclosure," House Committee on Interstate and Foreign Commerce, Committee Print 95-29, November 3, 1977. Registrations filed were developed from a 1 in 10 sample of the registrations listed in the *SEC News Digest*, issues 75-1, dated January 2, 1975, through 75-250, dated December 30, 1975.

investors from price manipulation, and to protect investors from corporate mismanagement. All of these desired results would occur if indeed the corporate disclosure system improved the pricing mechanism for securities. Evidence indicates that SEC periodic disclosure has not improved the pricing of securities in the secondary market, and therefore the benefits that would flow from improved pricing have not materialized. Pricing of newly issued securities suggests that the supposed pricing improvement after the enactment of the SEC's registration program is weak and statistically insignificant.

Our estimate of SEC periodic disclosure cost is $213 million and for the 1975 new issue disclosure $193 million. The known biases in these estimates are all on the conservative side, so that true costs of SEC corporate disclosure would perhaps be much higher than our total estimate of $406 million. Taking into account the conservative nature of these estimates and the inflation rate since 1975, the 1980 costs of SEC-mandated disclosure are probably in excess of $1 billion.[36]

From the public interest viewpoint the economic case for our current mandatory disclosure system is extremely weak. On this basis alone the system could be dismantled, or at least severely modified, to effect a sufficient reduction in the costs it imposes on the private sector. Yet all the current initiatives relating to the corporate disclosure system are designed to expand it and further increase its costs.

The prospects for substantial cost-reducing modification in our corporate disclosure system are likewise slim when viewed from the perspective of the economics of regulation. Two relatively small, well-organized groups have strong and understandable interests in seeing that the SEC corporate system is preserved and expanded, namely, professionals who produce the disclosure documents and who receive them free. Those who pay for the system—corporate owners, suppliers, customers, and managers—rarely are aware of paying anything for it, let alone how much. Since the regulatory tax per person is small, they have little incentive to organize in opposition to the system. Hence their interests are underrepresented when policies determining the size and nature of the corporate disclosure system are set. However, in special situations where the disclosure system impacts heavily on a small, well-defined segment of the corporate-issuer community, some organized resistance to disclosure regulation has taken place. For example, the oil and gas industry and the venture capitalists have organized and influenced the shape of disclosure requirements affecting their interests.

Chapter 4

Deregulation of the NYSE Fixed Commission Rate Structure

Taxation by Regulation . . . one of the functions of regulation is to perform distributive and allocative chores usually associated with the taxing or financial branch of government.

Richard A. Posner,
Bell Journal of Economics and Management Science,
(Spring 1971)

The deregulation of the NYSE fixed commission rate structure by the SEC represents one of the few efforts in recent years to turn the tide against the growth of regulation. The NYSE fixed commission structure often was described as a pillar of the U.S. capital market system, a foundation upon which the U.S. stock market drew its strength. Doing away with this form of price fixing did not come easily for the securities industry, the exchanges, or the SEC. We examined the forces that led to the deregulation and their implications for the affected groups, first by the regulatory structure and then by the deregulation process.

Throughout the period leading up to the deregulation of the fixed commission rate structure, groups with special interests became active in the political arena. The deregulation process involved a number of regulatory hearings and bitter arguments, turf battles between federal agencies and the groups regulated by the SEC.

4.1 Background

Since it was founded in 1792, the NYSE has had a minimum fixed commission rate structure, and as a condition of membership all members are required to charge their public customers at least the fixed rate for brokerage transactions. In the early years of the fixed rate structure, the minimum commission rate was set as a percent of the par value of the stock. By the twentieth century the rate was in cents per share, regardless of the size of the transaction. Only much later did the structure allow a lower rate for a larger dollar value of trade and eventually for larger transactions measured by number of shares.

Since the pressures that led to the deregulation primarily were felt in the 1960s and early 1970s, we will concentrate on the rate structures and events of that period. Table 4.1 presents the NYSE minimum commission rate schedules in effect after 1959. In the 1959 schedule some reduction in commission cost was allowed for higher priced transactions but not for multiple round-lot transactions. Thus from 1959 to 1968 the schedule recognized some scale economies for share price but not scale economies for transaction size, as measured by number of shares per trade.

In 1968 some commission reduction was allowed for large transactions. A lower commission schedule for transactions greater than 1,000 shares was implemented. During the 1970s several additional adjustments were made in the schedule to accommodate large transactions.

The Role of Financial Institutions in Commission Rate Determination
Throughout the 1960s and early 1970s financial institutions were becoming a dominant influence on the investor front, and their presence

Table 4.1 NYSE minimum commission rate schedules stocks selling at or above $1.00 per share

Effective date	Rate schedule			
			Plus stated amount	
	Money	Percent of money		For less than
March 30, 1959	involved	involved	For 100 shares	100 shares
	Under $100		As mutually agreed[a]	
	$100–400	2.0	$3[a]	$1[a]
	$400–2,400	1.0	7	5
	$2,400–5,000	0.5	19	17
	Over $5,000	0.1	39	37

[a] There is a minimum commission charge of $6.00 per transaction, provided the number of shares involved in the transaction does not exceed 100; and the minimum is not to exceed $1.50 per share nor the total charge to exceed $75 per transaction.

December 5, 1968   For orders of 1,000 shares or less, the 1959 to 1969 schedule applies.

For orders of 1,000 shares or more, the following schedule applies.

Money involved	Percent of money involved	Plus stated amount for 100 shares
$100–2,800	0.5	$4
$2,800–3,000	Compute as $2,800	—
$3,000–9,000	0.5	3
Over $9,000	0.1	39

Table 4.1 (continued)

Effective date	Rate schedule
April 6, 1970	Interim service charge: smaller of $15 or 50% of the minimum commission on less than 1,000 shares.
April 5, 1971	Part of order exceeding $500,000 negotiable.
March 24, 1972	Orders of 100 shares (not to exceed $65).

Money involved	Percent of money involved	Plus stated amount[a]
Under $100		As mutually agreed
$100–800	2.0	$6.40
$800–2,500	1.3	12.00
Over $2,500	0.9	22.00

[a]Plus following round lot charge: first to tenth round lot, $6.00 per round lot; eleventh round lot and above, $4.00 per round lot.

April 24, 1972	Part of order exceeding $300,000 negotiable.
September 25, 1973	Previous schedule amended to provide for an increase of 10% on orders up to $5,000 and 15% on orders between $5,000.01 and $300,000.
April 1, 1974	Orders less than $2,000 negotiable.
November 19, 1974	Additional increase of 8% on orders in excess of $5,000.
May 1, 1975	All rates negotiable.

Sources: NYSE, *Fact Book* (various years).

was especially felt as the rate structures were changed. Institutional share volume on the NYSE as a percent of total share volume increased from 25.4 percent in March 1956 to 33.8 percent in September 1961, 39.3 percent in March 1965, and 42.9 percent in October 1966. Although the fixed rate structure was changed in response to the increasing importance of this new investor group and their demand for lower rates, sometimes the response was too little, too late. The desire by the institutions to avoid the fixed commission structure gave rise to the development of new, nonprice competitive pressures. Regional exchanges and the OTC market in listed securities, the latter called the third market, were offering favorable execution terms to institutional customers, and many brokers circumvented the effective fixed commission rate by arranging for give-ups for their institutional customers. Give-ups are a form of nonprice competition whereby institutional customers direct that a percentage of their fixed commission rates be redistributed to third parties, thus nominally maintaining the fixed structure of commission rates. By developing these alternative arrangements, institutions initially found their own way of achieving competitive rates and did not need to seek the regulator assistance of the SEC, an agency that regulated them on other matters.

Both the SEC and the exchanges (whose members arrange the give-ups) were slow to react to the give-up question. As early as 1963 a special study of the securities industry was conducted by the SEC. The report questioned the practice of give-ups and recommended that a thorough investigation be made by the commission.[1] The SEC, however, did not act on the give-up question until a proposal to limit give-ups was made to the commission in January 1968 by Robert Haack, president of the NYSE. The NYSE proposal was prompted by concern about the erosion of the NYSE's market share to the regional exchanges. From 1961 to 1966 regional exchanges increased their dollar volume almost 250 percent, and their market share measured by dollar volume over 14 percent.[2] Further, regional brokerage firms had a competitive edge over NYSE member firms because they could allow give-ups not only to members of other stock exchanges but also to members of the National Association of Securities Dealers or any registered broker-dealer. The NYSE members by comparison were only able to give up commissions to other NYSE members.[3] Mutual funds and other institutional investors desirous of getting more for their fixed commission costs would direct their transactions to the regional exchanges or to non-NYSE members for execution and authorize that part of their fixed commission be given up to other broker-dealers who, for example, would sell their fund shares or provide them with research.

The NYSE foresaw erosion in their market share as institutional participation expanded. In their letter to the commission the NYSE board of governors asked for rule changes that would give the NYSE a more competitive position and stop the NYSE commission leakage to other exchanges and the OTC markets.[4] The NYSE also asked the SEC to force regional exchanges to eliminate practices that were affording them a competitive advantage. On January 26, 1968, the SEC solicited opinions on the NYSE proposals from the NYSE, American Stock Exchange (AMEX), the regional exchanges, trade associations, institutional investors, broker-dealers, law firms, individuals, and the Justice Department.[5]

The Justice Department as a Catalyst in the Deregulation Process

The Justice Department directly challenged the continuation of a fixed rate commission structure. They suggested that the SEC should: (1) determine the extent to which commission rate fixing is required in fulfillment of the Securities and Exchange Act of 1934, (2) eliminate all rate fixing in violation of the antitrust laws, (3) develop standards governing the extent to which rate fixing can be justified, and (4) determine the proper means for assuring equitable and nondiscriminatory access by nonmember broker-dealers to the NYSE.

In response to the Justice Department's comments the SEC announced that it would commence hearings into the rate structure of the national securities exchanges in July 1968.[6] In the release the SEC requested that the NYSE either provide for an interim commission rate schedule that would reduce rates for the portion of any order in excess of 400 shares or eliminate minimum rates of commission on orders in excess of $50,000. The NYSE submitted an alternative proposal on August 8, 1968, providing for reduced rates on the portion of a transaction in excess of 1,000 shares and prohibiting customer-directed give-ups. The SEC approved the revision in an August 30, 1968, letter from SEC Chairman Manuel Cohen to Robert Haack. The NYSE membership voted on the change, and it went into effect on December 5, 1968.

By 1968 the SEC, the Congress, and the exchanges had become involved in the fixed commission rate controversy. Concerned by an April 1968 memorandum from the Justice Department to the SEC, calling for the abolition of fixed rate commissions, the NYSE submitted to the SEC in August 1968 a study listing eighteen major problems caused by the foreseen destructive competition that would result in the absence of fixed commission rates.[7] The major points made by the NYSE in this study may be summarized as follows. First, the NYSE contended that the demand schedule for transactions is relatively price inelastic, so that any changes in demand caused by commission rates would not significantly affect the demand for transactions. Second, the smaller more efficient firms would be eliminated by the larger more inefficient firms. The study claimed the larger firms would survive because they are diversified. Therefore increased concentration would occur without greater industry efficiency. Third, greater fragmentation would result in securities-trading markets which would seriously weaken the primary auction market. Finally, the existing system of trading stocks, including the minimum commission structure, that had led to investor confidence could be destroyed if price competition were introduced, in effect predicting chaos in the financial markets.

On October 30, 1968, the Justice Department invited a group of economists to present their views on the advisability of fixed rate commissions. The Justice Department also commissioned Michael Mann to write a formal critique of the NYSE's report, and in his paper, entitled "Economic Effects of Negotiated Commission Rates on the Brokerage Industry, the Market for Corporate Securities and the Investing Public," Mann addresses each of the contentions of the NYSE and summarizes, "I would anticipate the continued viability of the brokerage industry after the elimination of fixed prices, with the only major difference being that prices will move closer to the actual cost of providing the service."[8]

The Justice Department continued its criticism of the NYSE fixed commission structure by filing with the SEC a memorandum on January 17, 1976, refuting the NYSE's economic and legal memoranda. The Justice Department argued that (1) the outcome of the *Silver v. New York Stock Exchange* case established that the Securities Exchange Act of 1934 did not exempt the NYSE from the Sherman Antitrust laws,[9] (2) fragmentation would not occur in the securities markets if commission rates were unfixed, since the NYSE would probably regain some of the market share that it had lost to the regionals and third market, (3) competition would eliminate the practice of give-ups and reciprocal business, while lowering rates and improving accessory services, (4) establishing negotiated rates would eliminate apparent NYSE antitrust violations, and (5) the SEC should take further steps to abolish the restrictive practice imposed on members of the NYSE that precludes them from making off-board transactions and oversee rule changes that would increase direct access to primary exchange membership.[10]

In May 1969 the NYSE defended its earlier economic analysis by submitting a report on "The Economics of Minimum Commission Rates" to the SEC. The Justice Department's January 17, 1969, memorandum and the subsequent testimony of economists who represented the Justice Department's position before the SEC were criticized by the NYSE on several counts. Specifically the NYSE charged that the economists did not offer any statistical evidence bearing on the unique cost and demand conditions in the brokerage industry, were unfamiliar with the securities business, and relied heavily on general principles not applicable in the securities business. Moreover the proposals and interpretations advanced by the economists were contradictory. The remainder of the paper offered rebuttals to the Justice Department's arguments and concluded that the securities market "is not an area where one experiments, tries a new system and reverts to the old if the results are unsatisfactory." [11]

The Changing Attitude of the SEC toward the Fixed Commission Structure

In March 1971 the SEC completed the *Institutional Investor Study Report,* outlining the then current and potential effects of institutional investors on the security markets. Among its recommendations the SEC proposed that all obstacles to competition, specifically the fixed rate commission structure, should be removed and that the interim schedule of fixed rates should be adjusted to reflect the actual costs incurred and services received.[12] Alarmed by the recommendations of this study, the NYSE's board of governors asked William M. Martin to prepare a paper dealing with, among other topics, negotiated commission rates. Martin's recommendations were submitted to the board on August 5, 1971. In his report Martin suggested that the negotiated rates should be cautiously experimented with before any action is taken. He generally agreed with the NYSE arguments regarding fragmentation.

Congress Steps into the Commission Rate Argument

When the Securities Investor Protection Act was signed into law in 1970, the congressional committees charged with the oversight of the securities markets conducted comprehensive studies of negotiated commission rates and a centralized market system. The complete studies of both the Senate and House subcommittees were finished in 1973. Both subcommittees concluded that (1) fixed commissions were a hindrance to competition and should be removed, (2) regional firms could compete with large national wirehouses in a negotiated commission environment, (3) the securities industry's ability to raise capital for its own use would not be affected by negotiated commissions, (4) negotiated commissions would lead to a more unified central market rather than cause fragmentation in that market, and (5) securities firms would be forced to focus more attention on costs and operating efficiency rather than solely on sales.[13] These two subcommittee reports formed the basis on which the amendments to the Securities Exchange

Act of 1934 were formulated and eventually passed by Congress in 1975.

Conflicting Pressures—Competition versus Cost Increases
During the early 1970s, while Congress was exploring the merits of fixed rate commissions, the SEC held hearings on the increases in commission rates requested by the NYSE. In February 1970 the NYSE recommended a substantial increase in commission rates on orders of 300 shares or less but a reduction in commissions on orders of more than 300 shares. Because of the weakened financial condition of the securities industry, brought about by stock price and volume declines and bookkeeping problems, in April 1970 the SEC approved a surcharge for the lesser of $15, or 50 percent of the applicable commission, on orders of 1,000 shares or less.[14] The SEC rejected, however, the proposal submitted by the NYSE to reduce the commission schedule for orders of more than 300 shares but decided that the commissions charged for the portion of an order in excess of $100,000 should eventually be negotiated. To implement this, in April 1971 the SEC determined that commissions on transactions in excess of $500,000 were to be negotiable. In April 1972 the break-point was lowered to $300,000.[15] This gradual process of implementing negotiated commissions was used because industry participants had never traded in a negotiated commission environment.[16]

In the meantime the NYSE applied for further commission rate increases in 1971 and 1973, both of which were not objected to by the SEC.[17] In December 1974 the SEC approved an experiment where commissions would be negotiated for orders below $5,000; for orders above $300,000 commissions continued to be negotiated.

Despite the continued allegations by the NYSE that negotiated rates would cause the demise of the regional firm, illiquid markets, chaotic market conditions, and market fragmentation, the Securities Act Amendments were signed into law on June 4, 1975. In line with the intent of the act and regulatory initiatives nonmember NYSE commission rates were made fully negotiable on May 1, 1975, and exchange floor rates on May 1, 1976.

4.2   Public Choice Theory of Regulation

The deregulation of the NYSE fixed commission rate structure occurred over an extended time period due to pressures from several interest groups, to the changing cost structure of the brokerage and exchange industry, and to a shift in importance of the two major consumer sectors of the commission market, institutional and individual investors. Existing economic theory of regulation goes far in explaining the deregulatory process that resulted in fully competitive rates for commissions. Specifically the formalization of the Stigler model of regulation by Sam Peltzman is particularly helpful in identifying and measuring the forces that prompted the SEC to abandon its support for the fixed commission structure and move the NYSE toward a negotiated rate structure.[18] That model, which we have called the public choice theory of regulation, allows us to examine the effects of changing cost and demand schedules in the regulated market for execution services (the price of which is the commission) and understand how and why the regulatory structure ultimately lost its support.

Political Groups in the Regulation Process
The Stigler-Peltzman model has as its foundation the analysis of the determinants of supply and demand for regulation. The choice of amount and type of regulation is the result of a political auction where the regulator serves as the auctioneer and the successful bidder wins the right to tax the wealth of the others participating in the relevant market. The regulator seeks to maximize the support for his programs and must balance off the support received by the beneficiaries of regulation against the opposition to the programs. Mathematically what the regulator seeks to maximize is

$$M = n \cdot f - (N - n) \cdot k, \tag{4.1}$$

where

n = number of potential voters in the beneficiary group,

f = net probability that a beneficiary will grant support,

N = total number of potential voters,

k = net probability that a person who is taxed (not in n) opposes the program.[19]

   As they organize, gainers and losers face transactions and information costs. The size of these costs must be weighed against the net benefits of opposing or supporting the regulation. This relative balance will determine the probability of support or opposition given to the regulatory program. These probabilities in turn have an impact on the size of the groups in the regulatory process. In general the winning group tends to be small, with large relative per capita wealth arising from the establishment, continuation, or abolishment of the regulation. The large taxed groups tend to be ineffective lobbying groups, because of the high information and organization costs associated with successful lobbying and the problem of free riders in large groups. Although there may be some economies of scale in lobby or special interest groups, diminishing returns to group size and the dilution of per capita gains or losses often render small groups more effective in the political process. Therefore the auctioneer (regulator) is likely to maximize his political support by concentrating benefits on a few and taxing a large group (who bear a small per capita tax and thus have little incentive to organize against the tax).

The most obvious beneficiary of the NYSE fixed commission structure was the NYSE, which is consistent with Peltzman's criteria for a successful special interest group—small, organized, and high per capita wealth at stake. Deregulation, to be consistent with the first part of Peltzman's theory, implies that the groups other than the NYSE in the commission production sector or in the consumption sector become relatively more important before and during the period of deregulation. Peltzman also uses his model of regulator behavior to explore several implications and special cases of the general model, some of which help to explain the forces behind commission rate deregulation.

Setting the Tax
When Several Different Consumer Groups are Involved

Since Peltzman drops the assumption of uniform taxes (prices) on all consumer groups, the problem is no longer simply group size but rather the selection of the overall structure of benefits and taxes. Where two consumer groups have different demand functions, the tax rates affecting one of the groups could be negative, in which case that consumer group actually would be subsidized. In fact for a short period of time in the late 1960s individual investors were subsidized, but substantial changes in the overall tax structure in the 1970s could in time lead to massive opposition to the fixed commission rate structure. The balance in the structure simply was upset by economic and organizational factors that shifted the support for the tax structure.

Effects of Production Cost
and Aggregate Demand Shifts in a Regulated Market
Peltzman also explores the effect on regulation of changes in the cost
structure of the regulated producers or the demand function of the
consumer groups. In an unregulated market we would expect the price
to be set to maximize the profits of the producer. In a regulated
market, however, the price is likely to be set somewhat below the
unregulated profit-maximizing price. As demand or cost functions
shift, we expect the price to adjust to a new equilibrium, but such an
adjustment would be different in a regulated environment than in an
unregulated environment. If a regulator pays attention to a dominant
producer group, then we would expect faster, more responsive price
adjustments for cost changes than for demand changes. This phenomenon can be observed in the attenuation of the fixed price structure, despite massive demand shifts by investors.

Differential Demand Shifts by Consumer Groups
Another situation Peltzman examines is where two separate groups of
consumers are subject to different prices. A demand shift in one
segment of a regulated industry can also affect the price in another
market segment. For example, while increased demand by group 1
may imply increased profits for the producer, which in turn may create
pressure for lower prices, that pressure could also result in lower
prices for group 2. This result is surprising in an unregulated market,
usually, when the demand by a group is unchanged, the price of that
group's products would not be affected. A discriminating monopolist
would price the products independent of demand in the other market.
The implication for the regulated market is that regulators tend to
spread the tax to all consumer groups, not just the group affected by
the demand change.

Summary of Hypotheses to be Tested
Although the Peltzman-Stigler model has many testable implications
for the securities markets, we have chosen several of these from which
to develop and test hypotheses of market deregulation in security
liquidity services. The price for security executions or the brokerage
commission was regulated until 1975, at which time the SEC forced
the exchanges to allow their members to negotiate customer commission rates. The Peltzman-Stigler price regulation theory then applies

mostly to the deregulation of fixed commission rates. We will examine and test the following hypotheses:

1. A regulatory agency is likely to concentrate the benefits of regulation on a small group characterized by large per capita wealth dependent upon the regulation and tax a large group whose per capita wealth is small enough that the costs of organizing against the regulation outweigh the tax. If a change in the per capita wealth distribution occurs, so that the tax becomes large enough, the interests of the regulator may be best served by abandoning the support of the tax structure that benefits a small group. Thus we must identify the groups taxed by the fixed commission structure and measure the changes in the tax over the relevant period.

2. If there are different, unique consumer groups affected by the rate structure, some may be taxed and others subsidized. Such a structure will please some and penalize others. In the case of individual investors and institutions, however, changes in the production function and tax structure over a period of time acted to erode the subsidy, so that both groups eventually felt the tax, and the balance of support for the tax structure was tipped.

3. If the regulation is effective, for example, serving to channel resources from the consumer to the producer groups, then we would expect that an increase in production cost is passed along to consumers via tax increases and an increase in demand results in a lower tax rate, so that the producer (the exchanges) receives some of the benefits, but in an amount less than directly proportional to the increased demand. In any case the rate changes due to the demand increase are not likely to be as prompt as those due to cost increases. In determining commission rates, the SEC acted to assure that the benefits of the demand increase are not completely concentrated on the NYSE but shared with the regional exchanges and, to a lesser extent, the investors. Further, cost-increase rate changes are granted rather quickly in comparison to rate changes prompted by demand shifts.

4. When the consumer demand in one group shifts, the other groups are also affected. In other words the regulator tends to treat everyone alike. We can examine whether increased demand in the institutional consumer group resulted in price changes for the individual investor by looking at the rates in the two sectors separately.

4.3 Empirical Test of the Transfer Tax in the Public Choice Theory of Regulation

The taxed groups in the regulatory situation are the investors. By paying commission rates greater than those that would be in effect in a competitive market, investors are bearing a regulatory tax. Individual and institutional investors have different demand schedules for commission or execution services.

Changes in Stock Execution Services
Demanded by Investors and Associated Commission Costs

To examine investor-trading patterns and associated commission costs, representative dollar trades for the two classes of investors were estimated, using average trade size and price per share for each of the kind of investor for the years 1960 to 1977. The average trade sizes, share prices, and the effective commission costs are presented in table 4.2. In some years actual share price and trade size were not available separately for individual and institutional investors. Actual data observations were used where available, and intermediate points were estimated by linear and curvilinear interpolative methods.[20] The actual and estimated data points for trade size and average share price are noted in the table.

The average value per trade for the investors was calculated from the average share price and trade size, and then the actual transaction cost was calculated, using the NYSE minimum fixed commission rate schedule for the years 1960 to 1974, as summarized in table 4.1. In 1975 to 1977 the commissions paid are abstracted from negotiated commission rate data for typical trades reported in the SEC's monitoring studies of the effect of the unfixing of commision rates. The "effective commission rate" is the commission paid as a percent of the principal amount of the trade.

As indicated in table 4.2, the effective cost of executing transactions has been lower for institutions than for individuals. That rate differential has of course partially accounted for the increased popularity of institutions.[21] By 1968 the value of institutional trading surpassed that of individual trading. The effective commission rates were lower for institutions than for individuals for several reasons. Institutions increased their average trade size and tended to trade higher-priced stocks than individuals. At the beginning of the period the average trade size (number of shares) for institutions was about twice that of individuals, but by the end of the period that ratio had increased to more than five to one. In the early years of the period examined no discount was given for number of shares traded, but the rate was somewhat lower, the higher the trade value, rendering some economies of scale to price. Since individuals tended to trade lower-priced stocks

Table 4.2 Individual and institutional commission rates for representative trades (fixed rates 1961 to 1974, negotiated rates 1975 to 1977)

	Average Trade size		Average share price		Average value per trade		Commission cost		Effective commission rate (percent of principal)	
	Institutions	Individuals	Institutions	Individuals	Institutions	Individuals	Institutions	Individuals	Institutions	Individuals
1960	200	93	$46.25[b]	$32.00[b]	$9,250	$2,976	$84.25	$32.55	0.911	1.094
1961	205	91	48.95[b]	38.68[b]	10,035	3,520	89.12	34.89	0.888	0.991
1962	(229)[a]	(95)	(48.00)	(38.50)	10,992	3,658	98.47	36.34	0.896	0.993
1963	256	(100)	46.90[d]	38.46[d]	12,006	3,846	108.67	38.23	0.905	0.994
1964	(291)	(105)	(46.50)	(36.08)	13,532	3,788	122.95	38.89	0.909	1.027
1965	(332)	(110)	46.00[c]	37.00[c]	15,272	4,070	139.44	41.25	0.913	1.014
1966	376	(115)	45.87[d]	38.20[d]	17,247	4,393	157.18	43.82	0.914	0.997
1967	(426)	(120)	(45.65)	(37.00)	19,447	4,440	178.18	45.00	0.916	1.014
1968	(531)	(125)	(45.65)	(37.00)	24,240	4,625	222.09	46.88	0.916	1.014
1969	644	130	45.45[e]	35.82[c]	29,270	4,657	268.71	47.99	0.918	1.030
1970	(679)	(151)	(39.00)	(25.00)	26,481	3,775	276.42	62.57	1.0438	1.657
1971	713	172	40.31[f]	27.94[f]	28,741	4,806	294.18	71.71	1.0236	1.492
1972	(790)	(187)	(41.50)	(29.00)	32,785	5,423	320.54	89.95	0.978	1.659
1973	(870)	(201)	(40.00)	(27.00)	34,800	5,427	333.40	93.06	0.958	1.715
1974	950	216	35.69[g]	23.05[g]	33,906	4,979	384.82	99.71	1.135	2.003
1975	(1,079)	(231)	(35.00)	(22.00)	37,765	5,082	h	h	0.65	1.7
1976	(1,216)	(245)	35.30[g]	20.05[g]	42,925	4,912	h	h	0.50	1.55
1977	(1,350)	(260)	(35.00)	(20.00)	47,250	5,200	h	h	0.45	1.45

Source: NYSE, *Public Transaction Study* (various years); NYSE, *Fact Book* (various years); and SEC, "Staff Report on the Securities Industry in 1977" (May 22, 1978).
[a] Modeled data in parentheses. See appendix A for an explanation of the estimated data points.
[b] September only.
[c] March only.
[d] October only.
[e] Full year.
[f] First half.
[g] First quarter.
[h] The rates were not calculated, but rather the percentage rates were observed based on the SEC survey.

than institutions, individuals tended to have slightly higher effective commission rates.

Some economies of scale for share volume were allowed in the commission rate schedules after 1968, and the relative advantage of institutions over individuals with respect to commission rates was widened. From 1966 to 1974 the effective rate on the representative institutional trade increased from 0.914 percent to 1.135 percent, an advance of 24 percent. During the same period the effective rate on a typical individual trade grew from 0.997 to 2.003 percent, or an increase of 101 percent. In other words the spread between the individual and the institutional effective rate widened from 0.083 percent of principal in 1966 to 0.868 percent in 1974. The divergence continued to widen slightly after 1974 but appears to be beginning to stabilize.

Throughout this period, which was characterized by increases in the average trade size and in the overall volume for both groups of investors as well as decreases in share prices, there were also a number of changes in the commission rate schedule. Figure 4.1 presents graphically the average effective commission rate for individuals and institutions. Notice the points where the commission rate changed abruptly and the causes cited. Institutional and individual rates increased quite rapidly in the late 1960s and early 1970s until rates were deregulated. While the effective rate for individuals fluctuated in the early years, this group generally showed very large increases after 1970. Between 1966 and 1975 the rate more than doubled for individuals. Institutional rates did not increase quite as dramatically over this period, partially because institutions were able to take advantage of the scale economies built into the rate structure and because their average trade size continued to increase over the period. After deregulation individual and institutional rates fell, but the decrease was most rapid for institutions. Although we may still be in a period of adjustment, the rates for both groups appear to be stabilizing, or at least the rate of decrease is slowing.

Estimation of the Regulatory Tax
Imposed by the NYSE Fixed Commission Structure
The divergence between commissions paid during the fixed rate period, as given by the fixed rate schedules, and the competitively determined rates that would have been paid in the absence of fixed rates, provides an estimate of which trades were being taxed or subsidized. Since the commission rate structures changed over the period exam-

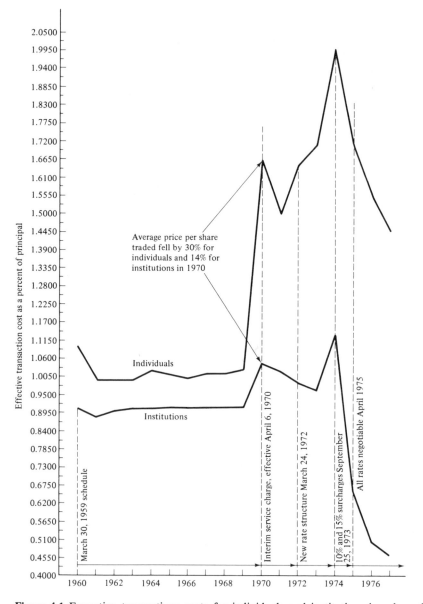

Figure 4.1 Expective transactions costs for individuals and institutions based on the average trade made in each year

ined, with increasingly lower rates allowed for large transactions, separate estimates of the tax rate were developed for different trade sizes. Table 4.3 presents actual cost in cents per share of executing transactions of 100, 600, 5,500, and 23,000 shares, assuming that the price for individual shareholders was $20 per share and for institutions $35 per share.[22] Again no economies of scale were reflected in the transactions costs for years prior to 1969, so the cost per share for the early years is the same for all trade sizes.

Also presented in table 4.3 are the estimates of the transaction costs that would have been incurred by investors if competitive conditions that existed in 1977 were in effect over the entire period. To implement this assumption, the cost structure applicable for 1977 was projected back through time, by adjusting the 1977 commission costs for the rates of inflation experienced during the intervening years. The average share price for individuals was $20 and for institutions $35 in 1977. The cost structure for that year was characterized by decreasing costs per share, as the size of the transaction increased. This method implicitly assumes that, by using the 1977 cost curve and only accounting for differences in cost levels, the relative shape of the commission production function did not change over the period or at least is approximated on a price-adjusted basis by the 1977 curve. In other words, there were no changes in either technology, capital investment requirements, or stock price that would alter the general shape of the curve. We will explore the implications of these assumptions in later sections.

As table 4.3 indicates, the actual cost of execution was greater than the estimated competitive rate for all cases except 100-share trades from 1966 to 1969. With that one exception then, we estimate that both customer groups were taxed by the fixed commission rate structure.

To determine the actual and relative size of the tax for individuals and institutions, the commission cost in cents per share was multiplied by the number of shares traded in each trade-size category.[23] The results of those calculations are presented in table 4.4. In general the aggregate amount of the tax on both individuals and institutions increased over the period but peaked in 1968. The cost of executing the 100-share trades was subsidized for the years 1966 to 1969. The amount of the subsidy, however, was small relative to the tax borne for intermediate-sized trades. It is also interesting to note that throughout the period the tax was not the heaviest for the 23,000-share trade

Table 4.3 Commissions actually paid and commissions that would have been paid under competitive conditions, assuming $20/share for individuals and $35/share for institutions

Trade size	Actual commissions (unadjusted, cents per share)		Estimated competitive commissions (cents per share)		Percentage inflation in each year
	Individuals	Institutions	Individuals	Institutions	
1960					
100	27	36.5	24.9	21.0	
600	27	36.5	15.6	13.2	
5,500	27	36.5	8.3	7.3	
23,000	27	36.5	2.9	4.4	
1961					1.01
100	27	36.5	25.2	21.2	
600	27	36.5	15.8	13.3	
5,500	27	36.5	8.4	7.4	
23,000	27	36.5	3.0	4.4	
1962					1.12
100	27	36.5	25.5	21.5	
600	27	36.5	16.0	13.5	
5,500	27	36.5	8.5	7.5	
23,000	27	36.5	3.0	4.5	
1963					1.21
100	27	36.5	25.8	21.7	
600	27	36.5	16.2	13.6	
5,500	27	36.5	8.6	7.6	
23,000	27	36.5	3.0	4.5	
1964					1.31
100	27	36.5	26.1	22.0	
600	27	36.5	16.4	13.8	
5,500	27	36.5	8.7	7.7	
23,000	27	36.5	3.1	4.6	
1965					1.72
100	27	36.5	26.6	22.4	
600	27	36.5	16.7	14.1	
5,500	27	36.5	8.9	7.8	
23,000	27	36.5	3.1	4.7	
1966					2.86
100	27	36.5	27.31	23.0	
600	27	36.5	17.1	14.5	
5,500	27	36.5	9.1	8.0	
23,000	27	36.5	3.2	4.8	
1967					2.88
100	27	36.5	28.1	23.7	
600	27	36.5	17.6	14.9	
5,500	27	36.5	9.4	8.3	
23,000	27	36.5	3.3	5.0	

Table 4.3 (continued)

Trade size	Actual commissions (unadjusted, cents per share)		Estimated competitive commissions (cents per share)		Percentage inflation in each year
	Individuals	Institutions	Individuals	Institutions	
1968					4.20
100	27	36.5	29.3	24.7	
600	27	36.5	18.4	15.5	
5,500	27	36.5	9.8	8.6	
23,000	27	36.5	3.4	5.2	
1969					5.37
100	27	36.5	30.85	26.0	
600	27	36.5	19.4	16.3	
5,500	14	20.5	10.3	9.1	
23,000	14	20.5	3.6	5.4	
1970					5.92
100	40.5	51.5	32.7	27.6	
600	29.5	39.0	20.5	17.3	
5,500	14	20.5	10.9	9.6	
23,000	14	20.5	3.8	5.8	
1971					4.30
100	40.5	51.5	34.1	28.7	
600	29.5	39.0	21.4	18.0	
5,500	14	20.5	11.4	10.0	
23,000	14	20.5	4.0	6.0	
1972					3.30
100	38	54	35.2	29.7	
600	28	41	22.1	18.6	
5,500	15	21	11.7	10.4	
23,000	8	14	4.1	6.2	
1973					6.23
100	38	54	37.4	31.5	
600	28	41	23.5	19.8	
5,500	15	21	12.5	11.0	
23,000	8	14	4.4	6.6	
1974					10.97
100	42	59	41.5	35.0	
600	32	47	26.0	22.0	
5,500	17	24	13.8	12.2	
23,000	9	15	4.9	7.3	
1975 (negotiable)					9.14
100	51	54	45.3	38.2	
600	32	37	28.4	24.0	
5,500	18	22	15.1	13.3	
23,000	6	12	5.3	8.0	

Table 4.3 (continued)

Trade size	Actual commissions (unadjusted, cents per share)		Estimated competitive commissions (cents per share)		Percentage inflation in each year
	Individuals	Institutions	Individuals	Institutions	
1976 (negotiable)					5.77
100	52	49	47.9	40.4	
600	33	33	30.1	25.4	
5,500	18	19	16.0	14.1	
23,000	7	11	5.6	8.5	
1977 (negotiable)					6.45
100	51	43	51	43	
600	32	27	32	27	
5,500	17	15	17	15	
23,000	6	9	6	9	

category. This was due to share price economies of scale in the early years and volume discounting built into the structure in the later years.

For comparative purposes the tax rates incurred by the two groups, were calculated as a percent of commissions, as presented in table 4.5. By our estimations the proportion of the total commission costs for institutions accounted for by the regulatory tax was 65 percent in 1960 and rose to 70 percent by 1967. On December 5, 1968, a new rate structure went into effect that allowed lower rates for trades greater than 1,000 shares. Since institutions were most affected by this change, their percentage net tax rate continued to decline slowly until rates were deregulated, and then they declined rapidly. For individuals the tax as a percent of commissions decreased slowly during the first nine years of the period we examined. The surcharge levied in 1970 and 1971 hit individual investors the hardest, more than doubling their tax rate for those two years. When the surcharge was lifted, the percent tax rate continued to decline. Based on these estimates, the regulatory tax was of much more significance for institutions than for individuals throughout the period, although the position of individuals varied considerably as a result of the changes in the rate structure.

The estimated tax was based on two assumptions. With this calculation the implications of relaxing those assumptions should be addressed. The first assumption was that price remained constant over the period: $20 per share for individuals and $35 per share for institutions. These prices were the average share prices for the year 1977. For the years 1960 to 1976 the actual share price was consistently higher than the 1977 average share prices. Since the commission cost

Table 4.4 Actual and estimated competitive commissions paid by various trade sizes (all commission figures in thousands of dollars)

	Commissions of institutions				Commissions of individuals				Total		Total net tax
	Actual	Estimated competitive	Implied tax	Implied subsidy	Actual	Estimated competitive	Implied tax	Implied subsidy	Implied tax	Implied subsidy	
1960											
100	18,189	10,465	7,724	—	75,126	69,283	5,843	—			
600	39,098	14,139	24,959	—	47,634	27,522	20,112	—			
5,500	23,884	4,776	19,107	—	12,657	3,891	8,766	—			
23,000	3,865	466	3,399	—	505	54	450	—			
Total	85,036	29,846	15,189	0	135,922	100,750	35,171	0	90,360	0	90,360
1961											
100	24,222	14,069	10,153	—	96,308	89,888	6,420	—			
600	52,894	19,274	33,620	—	64,026	37,467	26,559	—			
5,500	42,760	8,669	34,091	—	18,114	5,635	12,478	—			
23,000	3,707	447	3,260	—	897	100	797	—			
Total	123,583	42,459	81,124	0	179,345	133,090	46,254	0	127,378	0	127,378
1962											
100	19,465	11,466	7,999	—	87,609	82,742	4,867	—			
600	43,063	15,927	27,135	—	60,924	36,103	24,821	—			
5,500	42,410	8,714	33,696	—	18,462	5,812	12,650	—			
23,000	3,806	469	3,337	—	839	93	746	—			
Total	108,744	36,576	72,167	0	167,834	124,750	43,084	0	115,251	0	115,251
1963											
100	18,973	11,280	7,693	—	98,750	94,361	4,389	—			
600	42,896	15,983	26,913	—	72,066	43,240	28,826	—			
5,500	51,263	10,674	40,589	—	22,789	7,259	15,530	—			
23,000	4,714	581	4,133	—	1,169	139	1,039	—			
Total	117,846	38,518	79,328	0	194,774	144,990	49,784	0	129,112	0	129,112

Table 4.4 (continued)

	Commissions of institutions				Commissions of individuals				Total		Total net tax
	Actual	Estimated competitive	Implied tax	Implied subsidy	Actual	Estimated competitive	Implied tax	Implied subsidy	Implied tax	Implied subsidy	
1964											
100	21,345	12,865	8,479	—	100,446	97,098	3,348	—			
600	49,556	18,736	30,820	—	76,968	46,751	30,217	—			
5,500	70,901	14,957	55,944	—	25,316	8,157	17,158	—			
23,000	7,463	941	6,573	—	1,429	243	1,186	—			
Total	149,265	47,499	101,766	0	204,179	152,249	51,909	0	153,675	0	153,675
1965											
100	26,129	16,035	10,094	—	113,258	111,580	1,678	—			
600	62,420	24,113	38,307	—	90,748	56,130	34,619	—			
5,500	104,310	22,291	82,019	—	31,039	10,231	20,808	—			
23,000	14,973	1,928	13,045	—	1,955	224	1,730	—			
Total	204,832	64,367	143,465	0	237,000	178,156	58,835	0	202,300	0	202,300
1966											
100	28,247	17,799	10,447	—	119,069	120,436	—	1,367	10,447	1,367	
600	70,356	27,949	42,406	—	100,296	63,521	36,775	—	79,181	—	
5,500	136,526	29,924	106,603	—	34,461	11,615	22,846	—	129,449	—	
23,000	26,463	3,480	22,983	—	3,455	409	3,045	—	26,028	—	
Total	261,592	79,152	182,439	0	257,281	195,981	62,666	1,367	245,105	1,367	243,739
1967											
100	33,512	21,760	11,752	—	140,837	146,575	—	5,738	11,752	5,738	
600	88,248	36,015	52,224	—	124,804	81,354	43,450	—	95,674	—	
5,500	198,093	45,046	153,047	—	41,811	14,556	27,254	—	180,301	—	
23,000	52,545	7,198	45,347	—	6,859	838	6,021	—	51,368	—	
Total	372,398	110,029	262,370	0	314,311	243,323	76,725	5,738	339,095	5,738	333,357

Table 4.4 (continued)

	Commissions of institutions				Commissions of individuals				Total		
	Actual	Estimated competitive	Implied tax	Implied subsidy	Actual	Estimated competitive	Implied tax	Implied subsidy	Implied tax	Implied subsidy	Total net tax
1968											
100	33,623	22,753	10,870	—	144,027	156,296	—	12,269	10,870	12,269	
600	94,420	40,096	54,324	—	134,048	91,351	42,697	—	97,021	—	
5,500	240,424	56,648	183,776	—	42,576	15,454	27,123	—	210,899	—	
23,000	90,804	12,937	77,868	—	11,845	1,493	10,361	—	88,229	—	
Total	495,271	132,434	326,838	0	332,505	264,594	80,181	12,269	407,019	12,269	394,750
1969											
100	25,525	18,182	7,343	—	120,455	137,630	—	17,176	7,343	17,176	
600	80,287	35,854	44,433	—	118,945	85,464	33,481	—	77,914	—	
5,500	131,163	58,224	72,949	—	21,963	16,158	5,804	—	78,743	—	
23,000	70,060	18,455	51,605	—	9,469	2,435	7,034	—	58,639	—	
Total	307,035	130,715	176,320	0	270,832	241,687	46,319	17,176	222,639	17,176	205,463
1970											
100	34,785	18,642	16,142	—	165,798	133,867	31,931	—	48,073	—	
600	84,706	37,575	47,132	—	129,959	90,310	39,648	—	86,780	—	
5,500	134,661	63,061	71,600	—	21,963	17,099	4,863	—	76,463	—	
23,000	78,571	22,230	56,341	—	9,469	2,570	6,899	—	63,240	—	
Total	332,723	141,508	191,215	0	327,189	243,846	83,343	0	274,556	0	274,556
1971											
100	44,336	24,708	19,628	—	175,216	147,528	27,689	—	47,317	—	
600	113,132	52,215	60,917	—	152,557	110,668	41,889	—	102,806	—	
5,500	185,691	90,581	95,110	—	29,137	23,725	5,411	—	100,521	—	
23,000	120,674	35,319	85,355	—	14,543	4,155	10,388	—	95,743	—	
Total	463,833	202,823	261,010	0	371,453	286,076	85,377	0	346,387	0	346,387

Table 4.4 (continued)

	Commissions of institutions				Commissions of individuals				Total		Total net tax
	Actual	Estimated competitive	Implied tax	Implied subsidy	Actual	Estimated competitive	Implied tax	Implied subsidy	Implied tax	Implied subsidy	
1972											
100	44,438	24,441	19,997	—	155,723	144,249	11,474	—	31,471		
600	117,286	53,208	64,078	—	151,866	119,866	32,000	—	96,078		
5,500	195,855	96,995	98,860	—	41,984	32,748	9,237	—	108,097		
23,000	92,275	40,865	51,411	—	8,584	4,399	4,185	—	55,596		
Total	449,854	215,509	234,345	0	358,157	301,262	56,895	0	291,242	0	291,242
1973											
100	39,034	22,770	16,264	—	134,012	131,896	2,116	—	18,380		
600	106,850	51,601	55,249	—	148,669	124,776	23,893	—	79,142		
5,500	199,338	104,415	94,923	—	48,966	40,805	8,161	—	103,084		
23,000	86,851	40,944	45,906	—	8,079	4,444	3,636	—	49,543		
Total	432,073	219,730	212,343	0	339,726	301,921	37,806	0	250,149	0	250,149
1974											
100	31,794	18,861	12,933	—	110,954	109,633	1,320	—	14,253		
600	97,473	45,626	51,847	—	147,575	119,904	27,670	—	79,517		
5,500	215,946	109,772	106,173	—	57,106	46,356	10,749	—	116,922		
23,000	70,871	34,491	36,380	—	6,922	3,769	3,153	—	39,533		
Total	416,084	208,750	207,333	0	322,557	279,662	42,892	0	250,225	0	250,225
1975											
100	33,772	23,890	9,881	—	154,670	137,383	17,287	—	27,168		
600	94,156	61,074	33,082	—	199,072	176,677	22,396	—	55,478		
5,500	376,423	227,565	148,858	—	93,782	78,673	15,109	—	163,967		
23,000	80,345	53,564	26,782	—	6,540	5,777	763	—	27,545		
Total	584,696	366,093	218,603	0	454,064	398,510	55,554	0	274,157	0	274,157

Table 4.4 (continued)

	Commissions of institutions				Commissions of individuals				Total		Total net tax
	Actual	Estimated competitive	Implied tax	Implied subsidy	Actual	Estimated competitive	Implied tax	Implied subsidy	Implied tax	Implied subsidy	
1976											
100	28,881	23,812	5,069	—	149,582	137,788	11,794	—	16,863		
600	88,336	67,992	20,344	—	241,851	220,598	21,254	—	41,598		
5,500	240,769	178,676	62,093	—	120,706	107,294	13,412	—	75,505		
23,000	94,791	73,192	21,527	—	9,812	7,850	1,962	—	23,489		
Total	452,705	343,672	109,033	0	521,951	473,530	48,421	0	157,455	0	157,455

Table 4.5 Net regulatory tax as a percent of commissions paid

	Institutions			Individuals			Total		
	Total commissions	Net tax	Percentage net tax	Total commissions	Net tax	Percentage net tax	Total commissions	Net tax	Percentage net tax
1960	85,036	55,189	0.65	135,922	35,171	0.26	220,958	90,360	0.41
1961	123,583	81,124	0.65	179,345	46,254	0.26	302,928	127,378	0.42
1962	108,744	72,167	0.66	167,834	43,084	0.26	276,578	115,251	0.42
1963	117,846	79,328	0.67	194,774	49,784	0.26	312,620	129,117	0.41
1964	149,265	101,766	0.68	204,159	51,909	0.25	353,424	153,675	0.43
1965	207,832	143,465	0.69	237,000	58,835	0.25	444,832	202,300	0.45
1966	261,592	182,439	0.70	257,281	61,300	0.24	518,873	243,739	0.47
1967	372,398	262,370	0.70	314,311	70,987	0.23	686,709	333,357	0.49
1968[a]	495,271	326,838	0.66	332,505	67,912	0.20	827,776	394,750	0.48
1969	307,035	176,320	0.57	270,832	29,144	0.11	577,867	205,464	0.36
1970	332,723	191,215	0.57	327,189	83,343	0.25	659,912	274,556	0.42
1971[b]	463,833	261,010	0.56	371,453	85,377	0.23	835,286	346,387	0.41
1972[c]	449,854	234,345	0.52	358,157	56,895	0.16	808,011	291,242	0.36
1973[d]	432,073	212,343	0.49	339,726	37,806	0.11	771,799	250,149	0.32
1974	416,084	207,334	0.50	322,557	42,895	0.13	738,641	250,225	0.34
1975[e]	584,696	218,603	0.37	454,064	55,554	0.12	1,038,760	274,157	0.26
1976	452,705	109,033	0.24	521,951	48,421	0.09	974,656	157,455	0.16
1977			0			0			0

[a] December 5, 1968, new schedule for 1,000 shares or more.
[b] April 5, 1971, surcharge on orders of 1,000 shares or less.
[c] March 24, 1972, new overall rate structure.
[d] September 25, 1973, 10 percent increase for orders $5,000 or less; 15 percent increase for orders $5,000.01 to $300,000.
[e] May 1, 1975, all rates negotiable.

is an increasing function of the stock price, use of the actual share prices in the actual commission cost calculation would have produced higher actual transactions costs and a higher tax.[24] Further, had the estimated competitive commission cost been adjusted to account for higher (actual) stock prices, the estimated competitive commission cost per dollar of transaction would have been lower, reflecting the economies of scale to dollar value of the trades. This adjustment would further serve to widen the spread between actual and estimated commission cost and thus increase the tax. Our estimate of the tax then serves as a minimum estimate of the actual tax.

The second assumption utilized in the tax estimation was that the production function for execution services was the same as that which was in effect in 1977. Inflation or price level changes were accounted for, but had the price-adjusted cost function for broker-dealers changed during the period, our estimates of the tax could be biased. To relax that assumption, we would have to assume that either more or fewer economies of scale were built into the cost curve, the curve was steeper or flatter than the 1977 curve. Since by 1977 the deregulation had been in effect for only two years, the industry was probably still adjusting to the competitive environment, and thus the final shape of the cost curve cannot as yet be determined. Had competitive commissions prevailed throughout 1960 to 1975, in some years the curve would have been steeper than the 1977 curve while in other years flatter. The 1977 curve then seems to represent a compromise production cost curve and should not bias the estimates consistently in either direction.[25]

Deregulation and the Theory of Regulation
The regulatory tax imposed by the NYSE fixed commission rate structure eventually became so heavy that political support for the structure eroded. Our estimates of the increasing tax both in absolute terms and in relation to total commission cost is consistent with the Stigler-Peltzman public choice theory of regulation. The regulator is likely to set the tax rates that benefit a few and tax many. But, when the tax affecting the many becomes too large, then these taxed groups may protest, by avoiding the tax and organizing opposition to the regulatory program.

Indirect evidence that fixed commissions were imposing an increasing tax burden on investors during the period 1960 to 1974 is provided by the various schemes developed to avoid the tax. One well-documented method was trading away from the NYSE floor to avoid the NYSE fixed commission and other requirements. By 1975 regional exchanges, the third and fourth markets, and foreign trades accounted for between 15 to 20 percent of volume in NYSE listed stocks.

A second method of lessening the tax burden was to engage in nonprice competition. Familiar examples of this phenomenon include brokers providing extra services to clients, such as research, and the give-up arrangements, whereby a client directs part of the commission to third parties who supply other services.[26] However, barter and nonprice competition are not a perfect substitute for price competition. Barter is less efficient, since it requires negotiating in each case the mix of services, of a given market value, that are of the highest value to the recipient. This inefficiency could become a major consideration if there is very effective nonprice competition among brokers (which is quite possible) and the proportion of the commission to be bartered, given up or returned, becomes large.[27] Because the tax did not become particularly burdensome until the give-ups comprised a large proportion of the commission probably accounts for the length of time it took to accomplish the deregulation.

A third method of dealing with a regulatory tax structure that is not in equilibrium is for the regulator to change the tax schedule. Various attempts were made to change the tax structure in the late 1960s and early 1970s. Figures 4.2 and 4.3 show the shapes of the individual and institutional cost curves in terms of trade size for each of the commission rate structures in effect over the period. Discounts on very large share transactions were first allowed in 1968. Later other efforts were made to change further the tax rates faced particularly by institutions. The pre-1975 changes put the SEC in the awkward political position of mandating (called during this period "not objecting to") relatively high percentage commission rates on individual or small orders and at least condoning negotiated and deeply discounted commission rates for very large or institutional transactions. This behavior is consistent with the Stigler-Peltzman hypothesis that taxes generally are allowed to increase if the production cost increases, and the political wealth effect is empirically important. Price changes tend to be amplified when costs change, providing benefits to the small producer group.

The increases in the tax rate structure were only allowed to continue until the early 1970s. Then the pressure for a more competitive environment for the commission rate structure forced the SEC, as the

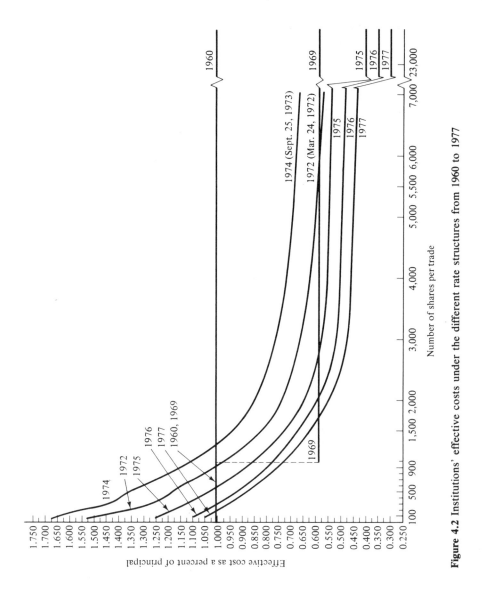

Figure 4.2 Institutions' effective costs under the different rate structures from 1960 to 1977

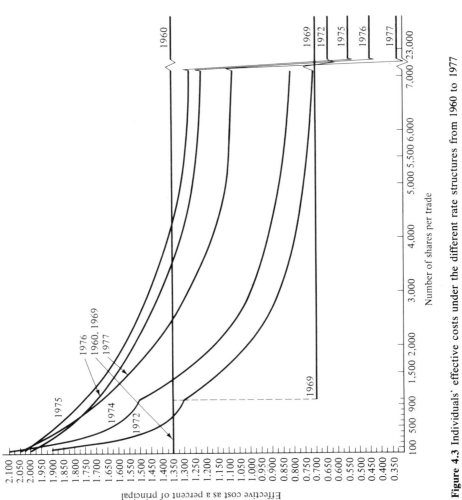

Figure 4.3 Individuals' effective costs under the different rate structures from 1960 to 1977

regulatory auctioneer, to drop its support for the tax system. But pressure may have also been coming from other groups in this political process, particularly those increasingly taxed, who now became more important than the producer group. As the tax became more onerous, and the relative demand for services of the two groups shifted over time, with institutions assuming more importance than individual investors, the ability to keep the tax structure in political equilibrium became politically difficult for the regulator to handle. If the political wealth effect is producing that wealth transfer from consumers to producers we should observe in Peltzman's words, an "attenuation of price changes when demand changes." [28] In this case the absolute value of the changes was not reduced until rates were made negotiable. Further, the tax as a percent of commission (see table 4.5) continued to increase for institutions throughout the 1960s, a period when their demand schedules were shifting upward. The regulator during this period does not seem as responsive to demand shifts as to producer cost shifts. Again we have witnessed a case in point theorized by Peltzman, "'regulatory lag' is likely to be longer when demand changes than when costs change." [29] By 1975, when rates were deregulated, the consumer group must have become politically more important than the producer group (the NYSE) in the SEC regulatory process. In fact the decreases in the tax as a percent of the commission after 1968 indicate that the SEC was beginning to be sensitive to demand pressures.

Another implication of the Peltzman-Stigler theory of regulation is that the taxed groups may be treated differently by the regulatory process. As the institutional demand for executions increased over the period, and as the rate structure was changed in response to that pressure (economies of scale to volume), the individual investor also was affected, but in a different way from the institutional group. In an unregulated market we would expect that the services for the two separate groups would be separately priced and insensitive to demand changes in the other market. Even before rates became negotiated, however, the tax as a percent of commissions for individuals decreased, starting in 1972. This observed phenomenon demonstrates what Peltzman-Stigler call cross-subsidization. The regulated prices are lower than those that would occur in a pure monopoly—the NYSE probably did not get the price structure it would have had as a monopolist. In fact the producer group subsidized smaller-sized trades and charged lower rates for larger transactions. On the other hand, the total structure of prices is different from what would have occurred in an unregulated market.

The important contribution of politics is to suppress economically important distinctions and substitute for these a common element in all prices. On the demand side, this means that regulators will tax profits by attenuating profitable price discrimination.

The incentive to reward or tax all customers for the peculiar characteristics of some has interesting implications for the structure of regulated prices. Not only will the profit-maximizing price discrimination be discouraged, but a peculiar form of price discrimination will replace it. This is usually referred to as "cross-subsidization" and, to the extent that this is not just another name for ordinary price discrimination, it connotes a structure in which an unprofitably low price for some is paid for from profits on sales to others.[30]

4.4   The Producer Groups in the Provision of Execution Services

The supply side of the market—securities firms, exchanges, and other marketplaces—had various degrees of economic interest in maintaining a fixed commission structure. However, by the early 1970s not all of these diverse organizations were earning excess profits due to fixed commissions. Much of the potential profits associated with the implied taxes shown in tables 4.4 and 4.5 were returned to customers through nonprice competition.

Securities Firms

The amount of support that any group gives to maintain fixed commission rates should correspond to the economic benefits they receive from fixed rates. This truism raises the question of why some securities firms, particularly the large, publicly owned ones, gave little support to maintaining fixed rates in the early 1970s or actively opposed fixed rates. There are two possible explanations: they were not acting in their own self-interest or they had no positive economic interest in fixed rates.

At least some indirect support for the notion that publicly traded securities firms had little economic stake in the fixed commission system is provided by the changes in their share prices, relative to a general market index, over the period when fixed rates were removed.[31] Despite large deviations from market performance over recent years in general, the performance of publicly traded brokerage firms before and after deregulation reveals no major change in their relative performance or in their risk level.[32] In other words, no significant change in returns or risk resulted when commissions were deregulated, as would have been expected in the case of a permanent loss of a monopoly profit stream. This observation is consistent with the notion that these firms were earning little or no monopoly profits from fixed commissions. Further, brokerage firms had developed a number of ways to avoid the fixed commission structure by executing on regional exchanges and in the third market.

Many other securities firms were harmed by the unfixing of commission rates, and some either went out of business or were merged with larger and/or more diversified firms. Even these firms, however, may not have been earning monopoly profits. The harm they sustained from the unfixing of commission rates may have been due largely to their specialization of capital and personnel in servicing the large-tax or institutional orders.

Exchanges and OTC Market

Exchanges were much more uniform than firms in their efforts to retain fixed commissions, suggesting that some exchange members and employees had a substantial interest in maintaining the fixed rate structure. A market evaluation of the exchanges, as reflected in seat prices, shows that exchanges suffered a large deterioration in their economic prospects over the period when rates were unfixed, a deterioration that has continued to the present time.[33]

The NYSE seat prices, for example, peaked in 1969 and since then have declined by about 85 percent to their February 1978 level of $64,000.[34] This decline has continued unabated throughout the period in both good and bad times for exchanges.[35] Reductions in floor brokerage rates on the NYSE, estimated at about 20 percent from the fixed rates by 1977, surely accounted for some of this decline in seat prices. But it seems likely that other factors diminished the profit prospects of the NYSE membership.

Regional exchanges and the OTC market may have benefited somewhat from the NYSE fixed commissions, by engaging in moderately successful nonprice competition. Although the Amex did not list the same stocks as the NYSE during this period, since many of its stocks are in similar risk-return classes as NYSE stocks, the Amex can be said to be an indirect competitor to the NYSE. Since 1969 the economic prospects for all of these competing exchanges have deteriorated proportionately even more than those for the NYSE. The Amex seats have declined over 90 percent to as low as $25,000, and most regional exchange seats were essentially free by 1977. The unfixing of commission rates played a contributing role in these declines.

The third market and the unlisted OTC market did not have fixed commissions, but both markets were providing services in competition with the NYSE and other exchanges: the third market traded NYSE-listed stocks, and the OTC market traded many stocks in the same risk-return classes as listed stocks. In this sense these markets competed with the NYSE and were partially protected from unfettered price competition by the fixed commissions on exchanges. Although they engaged in limited price and nonprice competition, the effective price of the services offered by the OTC markets may still have been higher than that available in an unfettered price-competitive environment.

Evidence that the third market has suffered in line with the exchanges over the 1969 to 1978 period is provided by the diminishing resources committed to it. By early 1978 the third market had virtually disappeared. In January 1978 Weeden and Co. announced that it was going to reexamine its commitment to third market operations, and subsequently it has merged with a more fully integrated firm. Since the third market largely was developed as a result of the fixed commission structure, its demise could be anticipated when fixed rates were eliminated and off-board principal trading restrictions for exchange members were left in place.

The effect on the OTC market of the unfixing of commission rates is difficult to measure, but some reorganization of that market is evident by observing market-making activity in NASDAQ securities. As indicated in table 4.6, the NASDAQ marketplace which encompasses most OTC securities has seen a decline in the number of market makers but an increase in the number of stocks in which the average market maker deals. Since the number of securities traded through the NASDAQ system has not decreased significantly, while the number of market makers has decreased by nearly 40 percent, we can surmise that the organizational structure of OTC market making has changed. On average in 1971 the OTC market makers were trading in approximately five securities. By 1977 that number increased to over seven securities. The increased scale of operation in this industry does not mean, however, that competition or the quality of services offered has

Table 4.6 NASDAQ Market Making, 1971–1977

(1)	(2)	(3)	(4)	(5)
December 31	Number of securities	Active market makers	Average market makers per security	Mean number securities per market maker[a]
1971	2,969	578	na	5.1
1972	3,454	628	5.6	5.5
1973	2,900	491	4.7	5.9
1974	2,564	387	5.0	6.6
1975	2,579	369	5.6	7.0
1976	2,627	365	6.5	7.2
1977	2,575	353	7.6	7.3

Source: NASDAQ *Factbook*, 1977 (NASD, Washington, D.C., 1978), p. 8.
[a]Column 5 = column 2 ÷ column 3.

been reduced. This observation is supported by the fact that the number of market makers per security increased over the period.

In sum, in a manner similar to the increased scale of operation observed in the brokerage industry, the OTC market making became more concentrated during the unfixing of commission rates. The unfixing of commission rates provided both brokerage firms and market makers (which in some cases may be the same firms) with the competitive incentive to experiment with different firm sizes to locate economies of scale.

4.5 Summary

The road to the deregulation of the NYSE fixed commission rate schedule was long and had many twists and turns along the way. The relative importance of institutional investors increased over the period, and the heavy regulatory tax imposed on institutions by the fixed commissions structure led them to exert considerable economic pressure throughout the process to change the fixed commission rate structure. The Justice Department, through formal submissions to the SEC and a series of dialogues with the NYSE, also placed considerable pressure on the SEC to force the deregulation of what it considered to be a form of price-fixing that could not be justified as exempt from the provisions of the Sherman Antitrust Act.

Throughout the period the cost structure facing the exchange community was changing. The exchanges were experiencing inflation pressures, but their commission income was not keeping pace largely because stock prices were declining. Faced with rising costs and decreasing revenues, the exchanges requested and were granted a series of rate increases. But eventually the pressure from investor groups, brokerage firms, Congress, and the Justice Department forced the SEC to abandon its support for the fixed rate structure. The political cost of maintaining a rate structure that benefited the exchanges to the detriment of consumer groups became too high, and the SEC acted to deregulate commission rates in a stepwise fashion.

The Peltzman-Stigler public choice theory of economic regulation which views regulation as a wealth transfer is particularly helpful in analyzing the breakdown in the fixed commission structure. According to that theory regulation results in a small group with a large per capita wealth dependent on regulation taxing a large group with a small per capita wealth loss attributable to the regulation. We reviewed the theory and developed several testable implications of it. Empirical testing required an estimation of the wealth transfer, or tax, from the large group (the investors, individual and institutional) to the small group (exchanges members).

The tax was estimated separately for individual and institutional investors for different trade sizes, by calculating the actual commission cost and then estimating the cost that would have been effective had rates been determined in a competitive environment. Very small trade sizes executed by individuals actually were subsidized for part of the period (1966 to 1969), but for much of the period small trades (100 shares) appear to be close to marginally priced. Namely, the implied tax for those trades is small in comparison to total commissions paid. Nevertheless the total tax as a percent of commissions for all trades reached as high as 70 percent for institutions in 1966 to 1967 and 25 to 26 percent for individuals in 1960 to 1965 and in 1970.

Throughout the period a number of adjustments in the tax structure were allowed by the SEC to reflect the changes in cost and demand schedules. The increasing proportional tax rates described in the previous section, however, are consistent with the Stigler-Peltzman notion that the regulatory lag is shorter for cost increases than for demand increases. Although in the case of demand increases some scale economies in the rate structure were allowed, the overall proportional tax increase until 1967 indicates that the producer cost increase effects had more of an influence on the regulator than the demand-shift effects. After 1967, however, the decreases in the proportional tax rate indicate that this regulatory phenomenon was reversed and that the SEC support for the NYSE fixed rate structure had eroded. The institutions were beginning to make their demands felt in the rate structures. Simultaneously the proportional tax decreases after 1967 that were most pronounced for institutional rates also were felt by individuals, which is consistent with the Stigler-Peltzman finding. Individual investors' demand for execution services increased very slowly over this period, although individual tax rates were being lowered by the SEC. In effect the regulator (SEC) appears to have been engaging in cross-subsidization from institutions to individuals.

Based on this estimation of the tax attributable to the NYSE fixed commission rate structure, we conclude that, although the rates were not fully deregulated until May 1975, the SEC effectively began to abandon its support of the fixed rate structure as early as 1969. The series of rate adjustments allowed for the fixed commission structure reflected opposing forces: inflationary pressures tending to increase rates were countered by a massive shift in the economic and technological factors affecting the various constituent public pressure groups which organized to lower rates. The rate adjustments can be thought of as a *tatonnement* process—a search for a new equilibrium rate structure as supply and demand curves shifted over time. The regulator choice problem thus was complicated, and the deregulation process was slowed, taking over seven years to complete, as the competing interests were factored into the ultimate solution.

Throughout the deregulatory period, however, we have demonstrated the general tendency of the SEC to abandon the fixed rate structure to the benefit of both individual and institutional investors. While some rate increases were granted during that period, they were less than would have been expected had the SEC continued to concentrate regulatory benefits on the NYSE and other exchanges.

Chapter 5

Market Structure

Solving a Nonexistent Problem? . . . In their extensive studies of the securities markets, neither the SEC nor Congress shows that the national market will improve the nation's capital-raising or allocating abilities. On the other hand, they both point to the fine job the markets have been doing in these respects.

Sidney Robbins, *Wall Street Journal* (May 7, 1979)

Considerable time and effort have been spent in recent years by the SEC, the securities industry, and securities lawyers in debating how to perfect a national market system for the trading of securities. The 1975 amendments to the 1934 act directed the SEC to facilitate the development of a national market system and to set up a national market advisory board to help the commission in its somewhat loosely defined task. Since 1975 some tens of millions of dollars have been spent on the development of a national market system with no result. The SEC has yet to develop a basic plan. Securities professionals have taken a critical view of this delay, pointing to present SEC-authorized market failures and calling this proposal ''Will-O'-the-Wisp.'' [1]

After nearly five years of hearings and rule-making proceedings by the SEC and its advisory board to develop the best market structure for the trading of common stock, the SEC has yet to make much difference in the development of a centralized market structure. That is not to say that changes have not occurred in the securities market structure but rather that the SEC has not been the driving force in these changes. The primary beneficiary group of the market structure status quo would appear to be the exchange community, a small, well-organized interest group with large per capita wealth at stake. Since the exchange community is fairly well organized, the public choice theory of regulation would suggest that the SEC probably has little incentive to initiate real change.

We have, however, observed changes in market structure, perhaps in spite of the SEC. We believe that the SEC does not control market structure changes for several reasons. The securities market structure is much broader than the scope that the SEC has been considering for a national market system (exchange-traded common stocks). A truly national market system would include stocks, bonds, options, and futures, some of which are not even under the regulatory control of the SEC. In addition, these and other competing instruments trade internationally—out of the SEC's regulatory purview. But of greater significance is the fact that shifts in the economic environment and certain technological breakthroughs have altered the incentives of market participants. These economic and technological factors are the major influences on the organizational structure of the market for the trading of securities.

Any movement toward a more integrated and expanded capital market is likely to bring about some regulatory conflicts within the SEC and with other regulatory agencies. Many of the regulations that now govern the securities markets were written nearly fifty years ago in the midst of a stock market crash. The nature of the instruments, economic conditions, and technology have changed drastically since the 1930s, and these early regulations are under some strain in light of all market structure changes and the development of new and competing instruments.

5.1 Background of the Market Structure for the Trading of Securities

Traditionally the secondary market for the trading of securities has consisted of two components: the OTC, or negotiated market, and the exchange, or auction market. Up until the 1960s all types of securities generally would "try their wings" in the OTC market, and, when they became active enough, they would move to a regional stock exchange or the Amex. If the stock volume continued to increase, and the firm met certain requirements, the stock eventually would be listed on the prestigious NYSE. In the 1960s and 1970s, however, the traditional roles of the OTC and various exchanges have been breaking down.

Unfortunately the records for OTC trading are much less complete than for exchange trading, and more data are available on stock trading than for other types of security trading. Although no consistent long-term time series of OTC stock activity are available, we have used several types of OTC trading data and have isolated the major technological and regulatory influences on both trading environments.

The OTC Market
An OTC transaction is any security trading that does not go through an exchange. The mechanics and form of the market vary, depending

on the type of security and activity involved. Security dealers make markets in OTC stocks and bonds—they stand ready to buy or sell the security. They effectively interposition themselves between customer buy/sell orders. The more active the security, the less interpositioning is required. In the early days dealers communicated with each other by telephones and runners. Now quotations to indicate geographically dispersed buying and selling interest are displayed through an electronic communication display system.

Compared to exchange trading, the level of the OTC activity has varied considerably over the years. The major influences on the OTC appear to be developments in technology and economic factors. Table 5.1 presents the dollar value of the OTC and exchange stock sales and the OTC proportion of total dollar volume for selected years. Beginning in the late 1930s OTC activity rises in comparison to exchange trading, generally because the OTC trading is more conducive to low volume stocks. Total stock trading fell off dramatically beginning in 1938, and exchange volume fell to a low in 1942 (see table 5.5 for exchange volume).

In one of the first studies of the OTC market, Irwin Friend noted that the increased activity of the OTC market followed the establishment of the SEC, and he attributed much of its growth to the SEC.[2] Friend's reasons for reduced exchange activity, relative to the OTC

Table 5.1 Over-the-counter and exchange sales of outstanding corporate stock for selected years, 1920 to 1961 (in billions of dollars)

| | Dollar value sales of corporate stock | | | OTC as a percent of total |
	OTC[a]	Exchange	Total	
1920	2.5	36.5	39.0	6
1926	3.5	49.5	53.0	7
1929	22.0	135.0	157.0	14
1935	2.1	15.4	17.5	12
1937	5.6	21.0	26.6	21
1939	3.4	11.4	14.8	23
1946	10.5	18.7	29.2	36
1948	6.7	12.9	19.6	34
1949	5.0	10.7	15.7	32
1955	14.2	37.9	52.1	27
1961	38.9	63.8	102.7	38

Source: Irwin Friend, *Activity on Over-the-Counter Markets*, (Philadelphia: University of Pennsylvania Press, 1951), p. 9; Securities and Exchange Commission, *Report of the Special Study of Securities Markets*, pt. 2, (Washington, D.C., 1963), p. 547.
[a]The period 1920 to 1949 estimated from stock transfer taxes paid by Friend; 1955 and 1961 estimated from the Special Study questionnaire.

activity, included (1) the general restrictiveness of exchange rules, (2) changes in the tax laws that reduced short-term gain profitability (short-term trading being viewed as more popular on the exchanges than over the counter because of its liquidity), (3) improved communication systems, and (4) less attractive trading margins in exchange stocks than the OTC stocks, making the OTC stocks more attractive for broker-dealers to push.

Total stock volume continued to increase throughout the 1950s, and the role of the OTC market did not seem to change significantly during this period. Another way of comparing the OTC's and the exchange's success is to examine the value of exchange-listed stock and unlisted stock. Table 5.2 presents the market value of shares listed on the Amex, the NYSE, other regional exchanges, and unlisted stock. The relative market value of the OTC stock did not change very much throughout the 1950s but increased significantly in the 1960s.

The largest change for the OTC market came in the 1970s with the introduction of NASDAQ, the National Association of Security Dealers Automated Quotation system. The NASDAQ system allows the

Table 5.2 The market value of the outstanding stock of domestic corporations (all values year-end in billions of dollars)

	Companies listed on the NYSE	Companies listed on the Amex	Companies listed on other exchanges	Companies traded OTC	OTC as a percent of total market value
1952	118.2	12.5	3.1	28.0	17.3
1953	115.3	11.3	2.8	27.3	17.4
1954	166.1	16.4	3.6	38.0	17.0
1955	203.6	20.1	4.0	45.0	16.5
1956	214.5	23.0	3.8	46.0	16.0
1957	192.1	19.3	3.1	44.0	16.8
1958	271.8	24.1	4.3	59.0	16.4
1959	302.6	19.1	4.2	66.0	16.8
1960	302.1	18.0	4.1	69.1	17.6
1961	381.7	25.4	5.3	105.8	20.4
1962	339.9	17.7	4.0	90.1	19.9
1963	404.2	18.9	4.3	98.8	18.8
1964	465.7	19.9	4.3	120.8	19.8
1965	528.5	21.3	4.7	137.3	19.8
1966	474.2	19.4	4.0	131.4	20.9
1967	595.4	32.5	4.0	172.0	21.4
1968	680.1	49.6	5.1	220.7	23.1

Source: Adapted from U.S., Congress, House Committee on Interstate and Foreign Commerce. *Institutional Investor Study Report of the Securities and Exchange Commission.* Supplementary Volume I. 92nd Congress, 1st session. House Document no. 92-64, pt. 6, p. 412.

Table 5.3 NASDAQ volume relative to primary exchange volume

	Shares (in billions)	As a percent of NYSE volume	As a percent of Amex volume
1972	2.22	49	201
1973	1.68	39	227
1974	1.18	31	248
1975	1.39	27	257
1976	1.68	30	308
1977	1.93	34	296
1978	2.76	38	279

Source: SEC Annual Reports, *NASDAQ/OTC Fact Book*, 1977, 1978.

OTC dealers to advertise their bids and offers to each other via a cathode-ray tube (CRT) which reduces the interdealer communication cost considerably. The impact of this system on market structure was terrific: it was the first effort to integrate electronically the buying and selling interests of geographically dispersed traders. As one Wall Street observer pointed out, "NASDAQ's impact on Wall Street was comparable to that of the atomic bomb on warfare; after it appeared nothing would ever be the same."[3]

The automatic quotation system provided a successful alternative to exchange trading. Many firms that could even qualify for NYSE listing status have chosen to stay in the OTC/NASDAQ system, for example, Anheuser-Busch, Connecticut General Insurance, Hyatt Corporation, and SAFECO. The NASDAQ volume relative to other exchanges has been somewhat erratic. Table 5.3 compares the NASDAQ volume with the NYSE and the Amex trade volumes. After only eight years the system became a major competitor to the primary exchanges. Although in the early years the NASDAQ faced declining volume, since 1974 its volume has been increasing. In 1978, as reported by the NASDAQ *Fact Book,* its volume was only exceeded by that on the NYSE. The NASDAQ market is now almost three times the size of the Amex stock-trading activity.

Since the NASDAQ has increased the amount of trading information available for OTC investors and dealers, it has lowered the risk associated with trading those securities. One research study measured the effect of NASDAQ on the OTC spreads and found that the spreads were narrowed approximately 10 percent by the introduction of NASDAQ.[4]

In some cases the OTC market has directly competed with primary

Table 5.4 Third market as a percent of NYSE volume

	Percent of NYSE share volume	Percent of NYSE dollar volume value
1965	2.7	3.4
1966	2.6	2.9
1967	2.9	3.3
1968	3.6	4.2
1969	4.9	5.5
1970	6.5	7.8
1971	7.0	8.4
1972	7.3	8.5
1973	5.8	7.0
1974	5.3	7.0
1975[a]	5.7	6.0
1976	4.5	na
1977	3.8	na
1978	2.3	na

Sources: NYSE, *Fact Books* (various years); SEC, *Statistical Bulletin,* March, 1977.
[a]Consolidated Tape Association began printing all NYSE stock transactions in participating markets. NASD recorded the third market transactions.

exchanges in listed securities, the third market. Table 5.4 gives the size of the third market activity compared to the NYSE. Before fixed commissions the third market activity reached its peak, with 8.5 percent of NYSE dollar volume traded off-board. Now that the commission structure has been deregulated, it is declining in importance.

The OTC market will probably always be used by investors to obtain execution services without going to an exchange. It is particularly suitable to the trading of inactive or local securities, and that function is not likely to change.

The Exchange Market
The exchange market network has undergone more drastic change in the last five years than in the preceding fifty. The technological and regulatory breakthroughs in recent years are still being built into the exchange network, and we can only begin to assess what the trading arena will look like in the future.

No matter how one begins to analyze the securities market structure, the central role of the NYSE (formerly the New York Stock and Exchange Board, NYSEB) always seems to dominate the analysis. The notion of an exchange was conceived in 1792, when interested brokers congregated around a table (the board) to execute bond trades. Thus came the term seat, when referring to exchange membership.

Throughout its history the NYSE has managed to outlive all security exchanges in the New York area except Amex, require its members to trade on exchanges, and, until recently, maintain minimum fixed prices for its services. The only major threat to the NYSE came early in its history in the form of the Open Board of Stock Brokers. The open board dominated the stock-trading market from 1864 to 1867, at which time the NYSEB merged with the open board to become the NYSE.

The Amex (formerly the New York Curb Exchange) has never quite competed with the NYSE on a stock-for-stock basis. Rather the Amex has specialized in stocks that generally would not qualify for listing status on the NYSE, but most Amex members are also NYSE members. This complementary relationship has its origins in a tradition that dates back to the time when curb traders and brokers congregated outside the NYSEB to trade securities that did not qualify for the board-trading status.

Thus in the early years of American stock trading, the regional exchanges could not be considered to be the NYSE's competitors. Such exchanges offered mostly execution services for local securities and also occasionally convenient executions (in terms of location and timeliness) for national interest securities. Until cost-efficient communication technology became available, regional exchanges could best provide execution services when geographical location was a factor in the cost of execution. With improved communication systems regional exchanges have increasingly become directly competitive with the NYSE. In 1940, recognizing the competitive potential of the regionals, the NYSE proposed a rule that would have prevented the members of NYSE to do business on exchanges located outside of New York City.[5] The SEC, however, did not approve the rule change, and the *Multiple Trading Case* is one of the SEC's landmark decisions concerning this NYSE proposal.

In the case of mergers in the securities exchange industry, as technological breakthroughs reduced communication and search costs across geographical distances, securities exchanges in major cities have tended to merge into regional services. Table 5.5 presents the distribution of stock dollar volume across various exchanges for the years 1935 to 1978.[6] In 1935 there were thirty-six exchanges, but by 1978 only nine remained. Regional exchange mergers have occurred

Table 5.5 Comparative volume of sales in dollar value on national securities exchanges (as percent of total for all exchanges)

			National			East–northeast				Other	
	Total exchanges	Dollar volume ($1,000)	NYSE	Amex	Total	Phil.	Balt.	Wash.	BSE	%	No.
1	2	3	4	5	6	7	8	9	10	11	12
1935	36	15,396,139	84.64	7.83	94.47	0.64	0.04	—	1.34	0.07	7
1936	35	23,640,431	86.24	8.69	94.93	0.54	0.06	0.01	1.05	0.05	7
1937	33	21,023,865	87.85	7.56	95.41	0.52	0.07	0.01	1.10	0.04	6
1938	31	12,345,419	89.24	5.57	94.81	0.68	0.04	—	1.51	0.03	5
1939	26	11,434,528	87.20	6.56	93.76	0.70	0.12	—	1.70	0.03	3
1940	25	8,419,772	85.17	7.68	92.85	0.81	0.09	—	1.91	0.04	2
1941	25	6,248,055	84.14	7.45	91.59	0.99	0.11	—	2.27	0.07	2
1942	24	4,314,294	85.16	6.60	91.76	0.87	0.09	—	2.33	0.06	2
1943	24	9,033,907	84.93	8.90	93.83	0.59	0.21	—	1.30	0.03	2
1944	24	9,310,149	84.14	9.30	93.44	0.72	0.05	0.01	1.29	0.04	2
1945	24	16,284,552	82.75	10.81	93.56	0.81	0.01	—	1.16	0.03	2
1946	23	18,828,477	82.65	10.73	93.38	0.78	0.01	—	1.23	0.08	2
1947	23	11,596,806	84.01	8.77	92.78	0.90	—	0.01	1.51	0.07	2
1948	23	12,911,665	84.67	8.07	92.74	0.88	—	—	1.33	0.05	2
1949	22	10,746,935	83.85	8.44	92.29	1.06		0.05	1.43	0.07	2
1950	19	21,808,284	85.91	6.85	92.76	0.90		0.02	1.12	0.04	2
1951	19	21,306,087	85.48	7.56	93.04	0.86		0.03	1.06	0.05	2
1952	19	17,394,395	84.86	7.39	92.25	0.95		0.04	1.11	0.06	2
1953	19	16,715,533	85.25	6.79	92.04	1.04		0.02	1.04	0.05	2
1954	18	28,140,117	86.23	6.79	93.02	0.94			0.89	0.04	2
1955	18	38,039,107	86.31	6.98	93.29	0.90			0.78	0.04	2
1956	18	35,143,115	84.95	7.77	92.72	0.96			0.80	0.05	2
1957	17	32,059,020	85.91	7.20	93.11	1.00			0.70	0.04	2
1958	17	38,228,285	85.55	7.30	92.85	1.00			0.69	0.03	2
1959	17	51,863,624	83.76	9.29	93.05	1.31			0.60	0.02	2
1960	16	45,218,847	83.85	9.20	93.05	1.20			0.59	0.02	2
1961	17	63,802,451	82.41	10.58	92.99	1.19			0.41	0.02	3
1962	17	54,732,076	86.33	6.87	93.20	1.01			0.39	0.01	3
1963	17	64,320,192	85.24	7.31	92.55	1.37			0.40	0.02	3
1964	17	72,148,994	83.61	8.19	91.80	1.47			0.41	0.01	3
1965	16	89,225,194	82.04	9.65	91.69	1.13			0.40	0.01	2
1966	16	123,033,926	80.12	11.48	91.60	1.10			0.57	—	2
1967	16	161,746,463	77.48	14.29	91.77	1.13			0.67	0.01	2
1968	15	196,358,393	73.83	17.71	91.54	1.13			1.05	0.06	2
1969	14	175,297,509	73.93	17.16	91.09	1.44			0.68	0.10	2
1970	11	130,908,725	78.73	10.90	89.63	2.01			0.68	0.03	1
1971	11	185,031,361	79.46	9.50	88.96	2.30			0.59	0.03	1
1972	11	204,025,685	78.27	10.02	88.29	2.59			0.77	0.05	1
1973	11	178,037,429	82.26	5.86	88.12	2.46			1.00	0.01	1
1974	11	118,249,300	83.87	4.27	88.14	2.04			1.24	—	1
1975	11	156,947,352	85.18	3.61	88.79	1.73			1.19	—	1
1976	10	194,968,675	84.40	3.83	88.23	1.69			0.94		
1977	9	187,202,557	84.00	4.56	88.56	1.62			0.74		
1978	9	249,257,272	84.42	6.10	90.52	1.64			0.62		

| | | | NYSE | Amex | | | Phlx | | BSE | | |

Table 5.5 (continued)

Midwest							Other		West		Other	
Chi.	Clev.	St. Lou.	MSP	NO	DSE	Pit.	%	No.	SFS	LAS	%	No.
13	14	15		17	18	19	20	21	22	23	24	25
1.29	—	0.02	0.01	—	0.40	0.20	0.03	4	1.05	0.34	0.10	10
1.32	0.02	0.04	—	0.01	0.31	0.20	0.04	4	0.79	0.52	0.08	9
0.97	0.03	0.05	—	0.01	0.24	0.20	0.04	3	0.78	0.46	0.06	9
0.97	0.02	0.04	—	—	0.37	0.18	0.04	3	0.73	0.54	0.04	8
1.59	0.04	0.05	0.02	—	0.34	0.18	0.06	2	0.76	0.61	0.04	6
1.98	0.03	0.06	—	—	0.36	0.19	0.07	2	0.97	0.55	0.07	6
2.47	0.05	0.07	—	—	0.33	0.21	0.11	2	1.14	0.53	0.06	6
2.29	0.06	0.08	—	—	0.34	0.23	0.12	2	1.09	0.62	0.06	5
1.92	0.05	0.05	—	—	0.30	0.16	0.09	2	0.73	0.70	0.04	5
2.03	0.01	0.04	0.02	0.01	0.34	0.15	0.10	2	1.06	0.64	0.04	5
1.93	0.04	0.03	—	—	0.35	0.14	0.09	2	1.10	0.68	0.07	5
1.85	0.10	0.04	—	0.01	0.33	0.16	0.07	1	1.19	0.68	0.09	5
1.61	0.15	0.05	—	0.01	0.36	0.14	0.06	1	1.30	0.96	0.09	5
1.75	0.10	—	—	—	0.34	0.14	0.10	1	1.40	1.13	0.04	5
1.83	0.11	0.01	—	—	0.39	0.13	0.11	1	1.41	1.08	0.04	5
		2.35		—	0.39	0.11	0.08	1	1.11	1.08	0.05	5
		2.28		0.02	0.36	0.11	0.08	1	1.23	0.83	0.05	5
		2.67		—	0.43	0.15	0.10	1	1.11	1.09	0.04	5
		2.83		0.01	0.46	0.16	0.09	1	1.05	1.15	0.06	5
		2.41		0.01	0.39	0.14	0.09	1	1.16	0.86	0.05	5
		2.44		—	0.39	0.13	0.08	1	0.98	0.92	0.05	5
		2.73		0.02	0.42	0.12	0.06	1	1.12	0.96	0.04	5
		2.69		—	0.30	0.10	0.03	1	2.00		0.03	5
		2.71		—	0.29	0.19	0.04	1	2.16		0.03	5
		2.60		—	0.30	0.11	0.04	1	1.94		0.03	5
			2.73		0.32	0.09	0.03	1	1.91		0.04	5
			2.88		0.33	0.05	0.04	1	2.06		0.03	5
			2.85		0.41	0.09	0.01	1	2.01		0.02	5
			2.73		0.51	0.05	—	1	2.33		0.04	5
			3.13		0.47	0.05	—	1	2.62		0.03	5
			3.46		0.80	0.04	—	1	2.43		0.02	5
			3.16		0.57	0.04	—	1	2.85		0.02	5
			3.09		0.44	0.03	—	1	2.80		0.02	5
			3.13		0.35	0.03	—	1	2.66		0.02	4
			3.41		0.10	0.03	—	1	3.09		0.02	3
			3.69		0.11		—	1	3.81		0.08	2
			4.02		0.19		0.05	1	3.76		—	2
			4.13		0.18		0.05	1	3.93		—	2
			4.57		0.21		0.07	1	3.55		—	2
			4.77		0.23		0.07	1	3.50		0.01	2
			4.65		0.13		0.17	1	3.33		—	2
			4.76		0.02		0.53	1	3.82		—	2
			4.80				0.75	1	3.53		0.01	2
			4.20				0.17	1	2.85		—	2

MSE   CSE   PSE   Inter-mountain   Spokane

Notes to Table 5.5
Sources: For 1935 to 1965: Robert Doede, "The Monopoly Power of the New York Stock Exchange," Ph.D dissertation, The University of Chicago, June 1967; for 1966 to 1978: Securities and Exchange Commission, *Statistical Bulletin.*
Note: Phil. = Philadelphia Stock Exchange; Balt. = Baltimore Stock Exchange; Wash. = Washington, D.C. Stock Exchange; BSE = Boston Stock Exchange; Chi. = Chicago Stock Exchange; Clev. = Cleveland Stock Exchange; St. Lou. = St. Louis Stock Exchange; MSP = Minneapolis-St. Paul Stock Exchange; NO = New Orleans Stock Exchange; DSE = Detroit Stock Exchange; Pitt. = Pittsburgh Stock Exchange; SFS = San Francisco Stock Exchange; LAS = Los Angeles Stock Exchange; PSE = Pacific Stock Exchange; MSE = Midwest Stock Exchange; CSE = Cincinnati Stock Exchange; (—) = less than 0.01 percent; ⌐⌐ = merger.

in the northeast (Philadelphia, Baltimore, and Washington), the midwest (Chicago, Cleveland, St. Louis, and Minneapolis-St. Paul), and the west (San Francisco and Los Angeles). The NYSE generally dominates exchange trading over the period, however, with its market share at its lowest point in 1968, 73.83 percent.

Is the NYSE a Natural Monopoly?
The impressive survival and dominance of the NYSE in the exchange market raises an important question about the power of the NYSE in the securities exchange industry as a natural monopoly. Is there evidence in the case of the NYSE of increasing returns to scale over the range of production and of some type of barrier to entry and/or price control? In stock exchanges minimum fixed commission rates and increasing returns to scale could be accounted for by (1) geographical concentration and specialization in securities trading, allowing cost reduction due to inventory, search, and information cost reductions, (2) lower dealer bid spreads when trading activity is concentrated, and (3) scale economies in the cost of establishing and operating securities exchanges.[7]

Robert W. Doede in a thorough study addressing the monopolistic inclinations of the NYSE examined the exchange's history and found that the NYSE undoubtedly passes Stigler's survivor test—it survived.[8] He estimated the pooled elasticity of total cost for five exchanges for 1955 to 1965. The results of the regression analysis indicated that "there are economies of scale inherent in the costs of organizing and operating securities exchanges . . . [and] that the long-run average cost function is negatively sloped."[9] Also the average costs of the NYSE were shown to be considerably lower than those of the other exchanges examined (Amex, the Midwest, Pacific, and Philadelphia Stock Exchanges). As Doede points out, if monopoly rents were available to shareholders, those rents would be capitalized in the seat price. By modeling expected profits to exchange membership, Doede finds that seat prices are consistent with the notion of capitalized monopoly rents.

Doede's comparison of the London Stock Exchange with the NYSE yields evidence of lower barriers to entry, more competitive commission rates, more competing market makers, and less stringent reporting requirements than on the NYSE. London seat prices are considerably lower than NYSE seat prices. Doede suggests, "A relaxation of the restriction on entry, the allowance of a wide range of discounts and relatively open, unpoliced competition among members of the NYSE would drastically reduce their monopoly profits, and thereby reduce the price of a seat." [10]

Doede's work has provided a foundation for analyzing the effects on market structure of technology and regulatory changes. Seat prices should be a very clear barometer of the relative welfare of different exchanges.

5.2   Exchange Seats as Capital Assets

Another significant advance in the study of the market structure for security trading services is the analysis of NYSE and Amex seat prices as capital assets by G. William Schwert, which also includes tests for the effects of regulation. [11]

Exchange seat prices represent the present value of future expected return from membership, and shifts in the profit outlook from either regulatory changes or economic factors are reflected in the seat prices. Schwert sees the behavior of seat prices as "consistent with the joint hypothesis that the market for seats is efficient in its use of information and that the expected percent change in seat prices is constant through time." [12] Schwert used many of the same statistical tests that have been used for testing the efficiency of common stock prices and found that seat prices exhibited many of the same characteristics as stock prices: (1) seat prices were serially uncorrelated over time, (2) the NYSE seat prices exhibit about the same amount of market risk as a well-diversified portfolio of common stocks (the beta was approximately one), (3) new information is assimilated quickly into the seat prices so that previously available information is not important because it is already impounded in the seat price, and (4) changes in seat prices are influenced by unexpected changes in stock prices and share volume, two important factors in brokers' profitability.[13]

The Effect of Regulatory and Other Changes on Seat Prices

Once he establishes seat prices as unbiased measures of expected returns to exchange membership, Schwert uses these prices to test the effect of certain events on the welfare of exchanges. Schwert tests the capture hypothesis of market structure which postulates that producers in regulated industries benefit from that regulation. This hypothesis is a special case of the public choice theory of regulation which attributes regulatory actions to the pressures of the groups that have a high per capita stake in the regulatory process, the exchanges as the producers of liquidity services. This form of the public choice theory has also been labeled producer protection. If the theory holds, the relevant regulatory agency is said to be captured by the industry it regulates, conferring wealth transfers to that producer industry through regulatory actions.

Schwert examines the two major securities regulatory changes for this effect on the welfare of exchanges: the establishment of the SEC and the deregulation of commission rates. He concludes that because of the SEC's regulations,

. . . an abnormal capital loss was suffered by NYSE and ASE seat holders in March, 1934. The capital loss was caused by a reduction of brokers' expectations of future profits by about 50 percent as a result of the 1934 Act. The data do not indicate that subsequent information about SEC regulation caused seat prices to recover from the stock. The capture hypothesis is not borne out by behavior of the SEC with respect to the NYSE.[14]

Schwert observed that economic factors were in no way the cause of seat price reductions. Rather, according to Schwert, the size of the SEC budget was related to seat price changes. Only in the first decade of the SEC's existence was there any statistical evidence that increases in the SEC's budget (assumed to be a proxy for SEC enforcement activity) resulted in seat price reductions. Thereafter increased SEC activity did not seem to affect the NYSE members' profitability.[15]

To test the effect of the deregulation of commission rates, Schwert isolated the seat prices surrounding commission rate changes occurring after 1967. That was the period when the Justice Department became active in the commission price controversy, and it seemed that a major regulatory change would occur. If the deregulation has an effect on expected returns to the NYSE membership, then seat prices should reflect that change around the time of announcement, which Schwert interprets as the 1967 to 1968 period when the Justice Department became active. The NYSE seat prices fell unexpectedly about 5 percent (annual rate) on average in the three months surrounding rate changes from 1968 to 1972. No such significant changes could be observed in the Amex seat price behavior.

While Schwert's analysis does not cover the period when rates actually were fully deregulated, the effect that Schwert documents appears to be continuing. As shown in table 5.5, the NYSE's market share of exchange volume increased from 78.27 percent in 1972 (the last year of Schwert's study) to 84.42 percent in 1978. In his several studies Schwert arrives at the same conclusion, "All of these findings contradict the capture hypothesis that producers gain from regulatory supervision at the expense of consumers. There is no evidence that NYSE or ASE brokers have ever profited from the activities of the SEC." [16]

Schwert's work contributes significantly to the analysis of the market structure for securities trading and provides a framework for analyzing the effect of SEC regulation on different types of exchanges. The NYSE and the Amex are considered to be primary stock exchanges. But regional exchanges can compete with these primary exchanges in trading the same securities or closely substitutable securities.

Regional exchanges may be affected differently by regulation, economic factors, and technology than the primary exchanges. As table 5.5 demonstrated, the total exchange volume of the regional exchanges has been declining. Many small exchanges have merged or gone out of business. The decline can be attributed to several developments. First, improvements in information-processing technology seem to have helped the primary exchanges more than the regionals. Second, the deregulation of the NYSE commission rates removed a competitive advantage of the regionals, namely, their ability to offer discount commission rates and more favorable give-ups or reciprocity services than available on the NYSE. With deregulation the NYSE members can compete in prices with the regionals. Finally, the introduction of the NASDAQ in the OTC market has provided issuers with an attractive alternative to primary exchange membership, a market that regionals have always dominated.

Table 5.6 Selected descriptive and regression statistics for the NYSE and the Phlx, 1929 to 1978 (semiannual observations)

1. Descriptive statistics

Seat prices	Mean	Standard deviation	Standard deviation/mean
Phlx	$ 5,601	$ 8,207	1.465
NYSE	$134,900	$111,446	0.826

2. Regression Analysis, Phlx $= f$(NYSE)

   Correlation coefficient (NYSE vs. Phlx): -0.773

Phlx seat $=$	0.065 (NYSE seat)	$-$ $31,960
Standard error	0.00346	603.43
t statistic	18.873	-5.297

Sum of square	Multiple R	R^2
Unadjusted	0.8856	0.7842
Adjusted	0.8843	0.7820

   Standard deviation of residuals 3831.78

To examine both the absolute and relative seat price positions of regional stock exchanges, we have chosen the Philadelphia Stock Exchange (Phlx) to represent regional exchanges. The Phlx has been in existence since 1929, and, although subject to some merger activity (the Phlx took over the Baltimore and Washington exchanges which in companion to it were smaller exchanges), we believe that little price distortion from the merger exists.

Table 5.6 presents selected descriptive and regression statistics for the NYSE and the Phlx.[17] We see from the normalized standard deviation that the Phlx exhibits more seat price volatility than the NYSE. The significant coefficient for the regression analysis that relates the seat prices of the two exchanges indicates that Phlx seat prices are a positive function of the primary exchange seat prices. The widely different scale of the two price series, however, is indicated by the large constant in the equation ($-$$31,960). That scale difference accounts for the negative correlation coefficient. While the Phlx seat prices exhibit more risk than the NYSE seats, if the prices are scale adjusted, Phlx seat prices seem to move in the same pattern as the NYSE seat prices. In effect, the Phlx seats are affected by the same economic influences or expectations as the NYSE seats. However, the regional exchanges do not appear to have participated in the total exchange volume that has increased steadily after 1974 (see table 5.5), which is consistent with the notion that improved technology and deregulation have operated against the regionals.

Table 5.7 presents the percentage price changes for several ex-

Table 5.7 Annual rates of change in exchange seat prices selected intervals, 1929 to 1978 (current dollars)

Period	NYSE	Phlx	CBOE	CBOT
50 years				
1/29–12/78	−4.0	−11.3	—	3.9
10 year				
1/29–12/38	−19.0	−31.0	—	−26.0
1/39–12/48	−5.0	−4.0	—	8.8
1/49–12/58	12.7	17.5	—	1.3
1/59–12/68	14.0	17.6	—	23.8
1/69–12/78	−17.5	−49.2	38.0[a]	31.8
Selected intervals				
1/29–12/42	−19.4	−34.8	—	−31.6
1/43–12/54	10.2	22.1	—	36.0
1/55–12/74	−0.9	1.6	—	13.5
1/75–12/78	0	−49.2	17.8	29.1

[a] For 1/74–12/78 only.

changes over selected intervals between 1929 and 1978 (the annual percentage price changes are given in appendix B).[18] From 1929 to 1942 the price change for a Phlx seat was −34.8 percent and for the NYSE −19.4 percent. The fortunes of the NYSE and the Phlx were reversed from 1942 to 1954: the percentage price change of a seat on the Phlx was almost twice the percentage price change of the NYSE. For the entire period the price change for a seat on the Phlx was lower than on the NYSE, but in neither case has the asset value (in constant dollars) of a seat holder recovered from the stock market crash in 1929. These observations are consistent with the findings of Schwert for the NYSE: the price for the Phlx seat decreased over the fifty-year period far more than for a NYSE seat.

Deregulation of commission rates has particularly affected the regional stock exchanges. In table 5.7 the annual price change from the beginning of 1975 to the end of 1978 is −49.2 percent for the regional exchanges, as compared to a 0 percent price change for the NYSE seat holders.

To demonstrate further how the Phlx has fared relative to the NYSE, the ratio of the NYSE seat price to the Phlx seat price was calculated. Semiannual seat prices were observed from 1929 to 1978. The standardized (relative to the mean) values are presented in figure 5.1 (the entire ratio series appears in appendix C). From 1928 to 1954 seat prices of the NYSE were quite erratic in comparison to the Phlx, although the relative price performance of the NYSE seats was

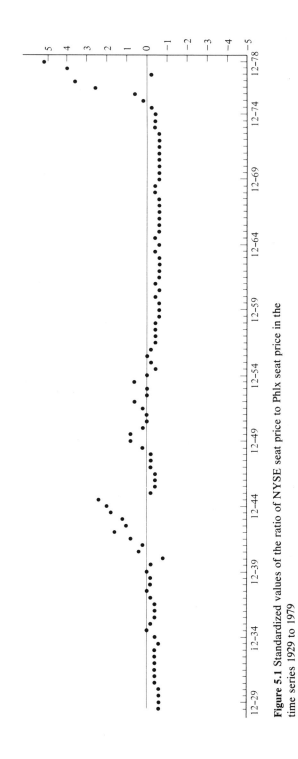

Figure 5.1 Standardized values of the ratio of NYSE seat price to Phlx seat price in the time series 1929 to 1979

stronger from 1941 to 1944.[19] Recall from table 5.5 that the dollar volume of total exchange trading was also erratic during this period. The stock market crash in October 1929 did not end the problems of the market. Approximately a twenty-year low in dollar and share volume was experienced in 1942.[20] Thus except for the 1941 to 1944 period few conclusions can be drawn regarding the relative performance of the NYSE and Phlx from 1928 to 1945. The relative price performance of the two exchanges shows no clear superiority of one exchange over the other.

Beginning in 1954, however, a Phlx seat appears to be a slightly better investment than a NYSE seat, at least until the end of 1973.[21] By 1974 the effects of the deregulation of fixed commission rates were starting to be felt, and the advantage of the NYSE over the Phlx is dramatic. The economies of scale are such that clearly membership in the NYSE is more valuable than in the Phlx. These findings are not inconsistent with Schwert's. By the end of 1978 the value of a Phlx membership had been reduced practically to zero. The ratio of the NYSE seat price to the Phlx seat price is five standard deviations away from the mean ratio for the fifty-year period.

5.3   The Future of the Regional Exchanges

The outlook for the regional exchanges can improve if the regionals make adjustments in the way they do business. The natural monopoly hypothesis of the exchange market suggested by Doede is true only in the sense that market maker risks, and thus price and cost structures, are minimized if orders can meet. In view of the developing technology for order execution services, there is no reason why the natural monopoly cannot expand to a geographically dispersed, but electronically linked, system.

We have considerable evidence that the exchange market system is moving in that direction. Already some regional exchanges have set up their own automatic execution systems to offer low-cost executions to customers: the Pacific Stock Exchange uses COMEX, Phlx the PACE system, and the Midwest Stock Exchange the MAX system. Such systems provide formula executions, priced off the last sale on the NYSE. Also automatic communication systems have been developed to integrate dispersed last sale and quotation information. Arbitrageurs no longer have to use telephones to keep the pricing systems coordinated between separate, disparate market places.

Low-cost execution systems that will facilitate cross-executions between geographically dispersed market places are increasingly becoming available to the exchanges. The Intermarket Trading System (ITS), generally defined as exchanges or the NASD, was pioneered by the NYSE to link electronically geographically dispersed market centers and collect third market trades. The Weeden Holding Company developed a computerized execution system, originally called the Weeden WHAM (Weeden Holding Co. Automated Market). The Weeden WHAM system has gone through several iterations (namely, RMS or RAM, Regional Market System) but has now emerged as the Cincinnati Stock Exchange (CSE), which is conveniently located in Jersey City. By creating access membership, the system can execute orders transmitted on CRT terminals from anywhere in the country, from an exchange or an NASD processor. Electronic systems such as these, while still in their infancy, may in time give the regionals a fighting chance to survive in the stock-trading business.

How does the SEC fit into the development of a natural monopoly for security trading? The 1975 amendments to the 1934 exchange act charged the SEC to "facilitate the development of a national market system." [22] Exchange and other markets were mentioned as composing this national market system. But the SEC has consistently acted to preserve the regional exchanges. In spite of constant urging by Congress, the SEC has yet to lift the NYSE Rule 390 which requires its exchange members to clear the floor of an exchange before taking trades off board. That rule has forced the third market into an exchange format (such as the Cincinnati Stock Exchange) to remain competitive. The SEC has mandated integrated sale- and quotation-reporting systems that give equal billing to the regionals for advertisement. [23] Ultimately the cost of such systems is passed on to the broker-dealers and customers. The SEC periodically threatens to put in a best execution rule that would require brokers to seek the best transaction price for their customers no matter where it is located or at what cost. The SEC, in granting options to the regionals and not the NYSE, ensures success to one business group at the expense of its major competitor.

These actions demonstrate the SEC's considerable concern for the survival of the regionals: Why? Most important, regulatory agencies do not like to see any of their regulated entities fail. Such failures imply regulator failure, that their regulatory and monitoring efforts have not detected the problems or weakness in an exchange's financial structure. Further, and consistent with Peltzman, if the industry is a natural monopoly, there is a tendency for the regulator to take actions that allow less efficient producers, in this case the regionals, to survive.[24] When the SEC acted to deregulate commissions, this hurt the marginal firms (the regionals) and perhaps forced them out of business altogether. The SEC would face criticism, court challenges, and even oversight by the Justice Department if the NYSE is left, by definition, a monopoly. The SEC's regulatory practice of granting the regionals stock options trading gives them a new lease on survival. The success of the options pilot programs actually surprised many, including the SEC, and strengthened the position of the regional exchanges. The SEC's moratorium on options expansion in 1977 served as a means of reinforcing the regulatory contract and regaining regulatory leverage over the regionals.

5.4 Summary

The market structure for securities trading has changed since its inception with the establishment of the SEC. The market structure is currently in a state of flux, which can be traced to three sources: technology, regulatory impetus, and economic factors. Improved communication, information, and record-keeping technology have affected the speed at which transactions can be made, have eliminated the disadvantage of geographical distance that has in the past prevented regional investors from making economically efficient transactions, and have improved the quality and quantity of information available to investors for decision making. These technological factors seem to weigh against the regional exchanges, however, because economies of scale have allowed the NYSE to regain much of its market share.

One major regulatory action in particular has harmed the regionals—the deregulation of the NYSE fixed commission rate structure. Removal of that fixed price system has allowed the NYSE to become price competitive with the regionals, and as a result the stock-trading activity of the regionals has diminished considerably.

Throughout the market structure shifts there is some evidence that the SEC is supporting the survival of the regionals. The regionals have been allowed to expand into new trading areas, in particular stock options, that have thus far been denied to the NYSE. The SEC has encouraged experimentation in certain types of electronic trading and linkage systems that permit the regionals to participate in an integrated stock market system. The SEC has mandated sale- and quotation-reporting systems that keep the regionals alive in the stock-trading arena.

More important than these SEC initiatives in the market structure area, however, are changing economic and securities market conditions. The development of new products to meet changing economic conditions is causing exchanges and traders to consider new ways of doing business. For example, the desire by some investors to participate in stock market risks and returns and by others to control the amount of risk that they assume in their portfolios has led to the development and success of exchange-traded stock options. Further, the continued high levels of inflation and the uncertainties of investments that depend upon foreign inputs are likely to enhance the success of stock options and other similar financial risk-shifting devices such as interest rate futures.

These new risk-shifting instruments are competing with each other in the expanded capital markets. The securities markets are rapidly moving toward a more integrated environment—the lines between different kinds of securities are no longer very clearly drawn. Stock options, which are close substitutes for the underlying stock, are competing with financial futures as risk-shifting devices. Financial futures are competing with bonds as hedges for portfolios, and futures and options have even been proposed for the same underlying asset—stock indexes and government- and agency-backed bills and bonds. We may well expect regulatory turf battles, as the SEC, the Commodities Futures Trading Commission, the Federal Reserve Board, and the Treasury Department compete to determine which will regulate these expanding markets.

Beyond the control of the federal agencies are the international capital markets. As more and more U.S. companies venture overseas, we can expect even more U.S. securities to trade abroad. The trading practices and market structures prevalent in those markets surely will impact upon our market system. The SEC will not be able to isolate U.S. capital market regulation from the influence of either competing domestic market structures or foreign trading systems. Thus in this expanded market structure the SEC will have increasingly less impact, as is likewise inevitable in the case of economic and technological influences outweighing SEC regulatory initiatives.

Chapter **6**

Conclusions

Economics and Economists at the SEC . . . It's been very hard for
us to recruit economists or to figure out exactly how to use them in
our kind of work, which doesn't involve the typical, purely
economic decision. So we haven't learned how to make the best use
of economists, and I think we should improve on that.

Philip Loomis, SEC Commissioner, *Barrons* (May 29, 1979)

Contrary to the traditional view of the SEC as the New Deals' most
successful regulatory agency and protector of investors, the SEC appears to be primarily concerned with maximizing support (net support)
for their regulatory programs. This practice results in a net benefit to
some groups and a tax on others, but more important it produces
regulation insensitive to the costs of programs and to an evaluation of
their effectiveness.

Problems with the expansion of the corporate disclosure system,
the fixing and the unfixing of commission rates, and many of the
actions and inactions in the market structure area are perpetuated
rather than repaired. But we have only touched upon a few of the
more obvious regulatory failures.

Part of the New Deal legislation passed in 1935, for example, gave
authority to the SEC to regulate various activities of public utility
holding companies. This program has remained small, in part because
the group that would have been taxed by this program was small and
well organized. The same general observation holds for the SEC's
regulatory programs aimed at investment advising and investment
companies (such as mutual funds), although these programs have expanded somewhat over the years.

The enforcement of the SEC's regulations ranges from an occasional
major fraud case, such as Equity Funding, where there was intentional
massive misreporting of assets and revenues, to a large number of
infractions in reporting or trading rules. Approximately 90 percent of
the cases are closed by a consent decree, which imposes no penalty
but merely admonishes the charged party not to violate the rules in
the future.[1] There are many interesting economic aspects to the SEC's
enforcement efforts. Some regulations refer to fundamental issues
concerning the nature of a stock price manipulation and what consti-

tutes evidence of such behavior. Others relate to the allocation of enforcement resources, the probability of detecting those who violate the rules, the penalties imposed on those who are shown to have violated the rules, and the deterrent effect that this has on reducing undesirable behavior.

While all of these programs are justified as being in the public interest, and designed to protect investors from unscrupulous individuals or some kind of market failure, the goals remain vague, and little effort is expended to ascertain the effect of the programs on the level of unscrupulous behavior or the degree of market failure. Overall the much simpler question of how to measure the program's cost is systematically not addressed.

A recent exception to this practice occurred in a program the SEC undertook to develop accounting standards, in conjunction with various private groups such as the Financial Accounting Standards Board. The issue concerned standardizing accounting techniques for oil and gas producers. The SEC staff and academic economists and accountants retained by the firms prepared an analysis of the effects on stock prices of changing these rules. Thus perhaps for the first time a systematic effort was devoted to measuring the impact of a rule change and using that information in the rule-making process.

Despite this exception, an apt description of the SEC's failure to measure the success of its programs or how much the programs cost society, who pays, and how the resources are reallocated is that of New York University law professor, Homer Kripke, who comments, "The SEC suffers today from the sin of hubris. . . . [which] means thinking what you do is the most important thing in the world and that more of the same would be better still."[2]

6.1 Corporate Disclosure

The corporate disclosure system is by most measures the largest regulatory program of the SEC. Each year well over 50,000 separate documents, many extending to several hundred pages, are filed with the SEC. The preparation and filing of these documents requires substantial resources, primarily in the form of legal services and accounting services.

The major articulated reason for the SEC's disclosure program is to make investors better and more accurately informed about corporations. Better informed investors in turn would improve asset markets and make them fairer in several ways. First, through their buying and selling activities better informed investors will lead to more accurately priced securities. Alternatively stated, securities would be efficiently priced with respect to a wider set of information. Second, better informed investors, and more accurately priced securities, will make it more difficult to manipulate securities prices away from their equilibrium or efficiently priced level. Third, because the information will be widely available, everyone more or less at the same time, not just insiders and professionals, will be able to reap all of the benefits of new information. With this so-called insider-trading issue the lags involved in publishing SEC documents and the fact that few private investors read them suggest that the disclosure programs have not succeeded in making information available to all at the same time.

The first two intended benefits of the disclosure programs would materialize only if the pricing of securities were affected by the availability of the information in the disclosure documents. Several studies of the pricing of securities before and after the SEC was founded are available. There is convincing evidence that the pricing of securities was not altered by the introduction of the SEC periodic disclosure programs. Other studies of the disclosure requirements for newly issued securities found some evidence that investors fared better after the SEC was founded than before, but these results were not statistically significant. We therefore conclude that the major intended benefits of the SEC's corporate disclosure system, namely, the improved pricing of securities, have not been achieved.

The costs of SEC disclosure programs have not been adequately measured. However, the Advisory Committee on Corporate Disclosure to the SEC made a survey of a small number of firms to assess most of the costs involved in the major periodic disclosure documents (10-K, 10-Q, and 8-K) and major new issue-reporting documents (S-1, S-7, S-14, and S-16). Besides being much too small a sample, the data collected contain a number of known biases. Most important, various overhead and start-up costs were excluded from the data. Then not all types of documents were included in the sample. The known biases tended to understate the costs of these mandatory disclosure programs. We were also unable to determine if the participating firms were representative of their asset classes in terms of the costs of mandatory disclosure. This, coupled with the small sample size, leaves a large margin for error in estimating the total costs of disclosure programs. We would hope that better data on costs would be systematically collected in the future.

Our estimates of the SEC's 1975 disclosure costs are $213 million for periodic disclosures and $193 million for new issue disclosures. If some allowance is made for the documents excluded from the survey, for the underreported biases, and for the substantial general inflation in prices since 1975, then the 1980 costs of the SEC's corporate disclosure system is probably close to $1 billion per year.

These costs fall more heavily on small firms, when taken as a percent of assets or of sales. In our sample of firms, for example, medium-sized firms ($100 million to $1 billion in assets) on average paid .09 cent per dollar of capital raised to file the S-1 form, while smaller firms paid an average of 2.7 cents per dollar of capital raised. Overall we estimate that registration of newly issued securities adds about .5 cent per dollar of capital raised, which is a significant amount compared to the total costs of raising new capital.

Significantly the SEC disclosure system is not the only, or even the major, way in which corporations make their financial and other activities public. Voluntary disclosure expenditures by corporations are much larger than SEC-mandated expenditures, probably about four times as large. Thus the practice of voluntary disclosure by corporations which was widespread before the SEC was founded has continued to play the major role in corporate disclosure.

We conclude that the corporate disclosure system is costly compared to its benefits, if any. A dismantling of the SEC's corporate disclosure system would not distort the pricing mechanics for securities or harm investors in other ways. It would of course lessen demand for certain types of legal, accounting, and other services, and it would benefit those who pay for this system now, including investors, by a small per capita amount. Short of dismantling the system, a systematic effort could be made to assess costs and replace costly programs with low-cost alternatives, such as disclosure forms that are much less expensive for firms to prepare.

6.2   Deregulation of the NYSE Fixed Commission Rate Structure

The NYSE fixed commission rate structure is as old as the forerunner of the NYSE itself. In fact the original Buttonwood Tree Agreement included not only a commitment to limit trading to the signers of the agreement but also to charge a minimum commission for those transactions. Although the nature of the fixed charge changed over the years, the NYSE was able to maintain the structure until pressures in the late 1960s and early 1970s began to put considerable strain on the cartel's fixed commission structure.

The fixed price system eroded economically in several ways, even before the regulatory authorities forced its final abandonment in 1975. As financial institutions became a stronger voice in the marketplace, and competition for their business heated up, pressure was put on the NYSE as the price setter to adjust commission rate structures to allow some discounts for large transactions. But even that adjustment did not allow enough competitive latitude for the brokers to compete for institutional business. That competitive pressure forced broker-dealers to develop varieties of nonprice competition, such as give-ups, reciprocal agreements, and over-the-counter trading of listed securities. As improved technology continued to lower the cost of executions, the size of give-ups relative to the total commission became increasingly large, and this barter type of compensation became increasingly inefficient. The support given to the fixed commission rate structure by exchange members was drastically reduced.

The size of the wealth that was reallocated by the fixed rate structure was significant. Except for a brief period beginning in 1969 for small trades by individuals, there was a tax for all sizes of trades for both individual and institutional investors. While the tax was small and dispersed among many investors who were basically unorganized, there was little opposition to the fixed rate structure. The SEC was not really pressured to change the status quo and in fact was encouraged to enforce the NYSE's rate system by the exchanges. The beneficiaries of the fixed rate system were the exchange members, a concentrated group with a high per capita wealth dependent upon the rate structure. The taxed group—investors—bore a small per capita tax, small enough to inhibit them from organizing to oppose the rate structure.

Changes in the economic environment, however, eventually tipped the regulatory equilibrium. As the tax system became increasingly onerous, the costs to organize and oppose the regulatory structure became less important. Other regulatory agencies and Congress joined in the opposition to the rate structure, and finally the SEC abandoned its support. Commission rates were fully deregulated by May 1975.

This change has put the regional exchanges at a disadvantage relative to the NYSE for stock trading, and the NYSE has regained much of its market share. At the same time, however, the SEC has given regional exchanges the franchise on options trading but has denied it to the NYSE. The role of the SEC as a regulatory auctioneer is not hard to visualize in the market structure area. The wealth transfer lost due to one regulatory action is offset by a gain from another. The entire auction process whereby the exchanges are the bidders for rights to revenue streams has influenced the shape of the market structure, and deregulation cannot be addressed without some recognition of the influences of various forces on market structure.

6.3   Market Structure

Until improvements in communication technology made possible low-cost information systems that could facilitate cross-country trading through broker-dealers, the market structure for securities trading was built around a series of geographically dispersed exchanges. Exchanges were an economically efficient method of bringing buyers and sellers together, and a series of exchanges was necessary because of the cost of maintaining on-line information systems for security price information. In the 1930s we had over thirty-eight exchanges in the United States. As communication systems were developed that would allow low-cost price information to be available on a geographically dispersed basis, many of these exchanges began to disappear. By the late 1970s, only nine exchanges were left.

For the trading of common stock the NYSE has always dominated the market for security trading. Brokers traditionally have felt confident that, if they channeled their orders to that exchange, they would have the best opportunity of assuring their customers of the best and most current price for execution. The search costs required to poll all exchanges for the best price is likely to outweigh the possible gains of a slightly better-priced transaction. Therefore the tendency to centralize exchange trading is a natural one. Only when communication costs were so high was it economically efficient to have multiple exchanges. Throughout the period since the SEC was established, which coincides with the improvement in information technology, the importance of regional exchanges in the marketplace has deteriorated significantly.

The dominance of the NYSE throughout its history prompted William Doede to examine the question of whether or not the NYSE was a natural monopoly. By natural monopoly we mean that there are economies of scale to trading fixed prices and barriers to entry. Unfortunately Doede's work was in the late 1960s and did not cover the deregulation period. The trends identified by Doede with respect to concentration of trading volume and declining costs as scale increased have continued throughout the 1970s. Indeed, the NYSE has been able to increase its market share since the deregulation.

To determine the effects of technological change and regulatory initiative on market structure, we examined seat price data for one selected regional exchange (the Phlx), the NYSE, the Chicago Board Options Exchange, and the Chicago Board of Trade. These data were examined from the period prior to the establishment of the SEC through 1978. The seat price is the major cost of entry to the exchange trading arena and reflects primarily the present value of future expected profits to owning that seat. Any regulatory or technological change that would influence that expected future profit stream therefore should be reflected in the seat price.

As Schwert has shown for the NYSE, and as we have shown for several stock exchanges, seat prices on all SEC-regulated exchanges declined after the establishment of the SEC. That decline is only partially explained by stock market conditions. By comparison the commodity exchanges which are not regulated by the SEC do not appear to have suffered the same deterioration of expected profits because of regulations. While all stock exchanges suffered absolute losses of expected income on account of the establishment of the SEC and the deregulation of commission rates, the regional exchanges appear to have experienced more extensive seat price deterioration than the NYSE.

Although regulatory initiative with respect to deregulation appears to have precipitated the price deterioration of the regional exchanges, that deterioration probably would have occurred more quickly in an unfettered, unregulated trading environment. In other words, had the SEC not acted for such a long time to enforce the barriers to entry and fixed price structure set by the NYSE, which also benefited the regional exchanges, those smaller exchanges would have probably suffered more and accelerated deterioration.

We have observed the SEC act to preserve the regional exchanges and promote competition among those exchanges. In an unfettered market we would have expected the low-cost producer (in this case the NYSE) to set the profit-maximizing price which would be lower than is the case in a forced competition situation. What appears to have happened is that the SEC has set regulatory barriers to keep inefficient exchanges in business, and the price of executions is higher than would be expected in an unfettered market. Once the commission rates were deregulated, we observed decreases in execution costs.

6.4   Future Directions for the SEC

The public choice theory of regulation has been very useful in explaining the existence and persistence of certain of the SEC's regulatory programs. The SEC has been the most successful in its disclosure regulatory programs, the securities part of the SEC. These programs are characterized by wealth transfers from investors and corporations for whom the cost is not great on a per capita basis to a relatively small group of processors, which includes securities lawyers, accountants, security analysts, and of course the SEC's employees. There is insufficient economic incentive by the members of the taxed groups to organize in opposition to this type of regulation.

The SEC has been less successful, however, in initiating regulatory changes in the market structure area, the exchange part of the SEC. The commission has typically viewed its role in the market structure area as promoting competition among exchanges. Unfortunately for the SEC the traditionally perceived competitive model, characterized by many competitors in this case, seems not to be the lowest cost model since economies of scale are prevalent in the securities exchange business. Regulation that attempts to maintain a market configuration that does not allow low-cost production will be under continual strain. If the regulations were relaxed, and prices fell, the dominant or low-cost producer group (in this case the NYSE) could recover some lost revenue from price decreases by increasing market share, so it is not clear that they would oppose deregulation too strongly. Moreover the investors will oppose the regulatory program since their costs (commission) are higher than would be in a competitive market. Although the NYSE originally objected to the deregulation of commission rates, their market share has increased substantially and they have since admitted that their earlier opposition was due to anticipated lost income that overstated their case.

More recent SEC initiatives in the market structure area have not been successful; for example, consider the case of the NYSE's Rule 390. Congress and the SEC have repeatedly stated that this rule was anticompetitive and should be abolished, but, whenever the time comes to remove it, opposition from concentrated groups who would stand to lose a large amount of per capita wealth (such as the NYSE and other exchanges) has always been strong enough to sway the SEC to keep the rule. Once the third market reorganized in an exchange format (the Cincinnati Stock Exchange), the impetus to remove Rule 390 lessened, and the market system has managed to reorganize itself around the NYSE 390. Even if the rule were removed now, little market structure change would probably occur.

It is not surprising that the success of disclosure programs and the lack of success in market structure initiatives provide us with insight for future SEC regulatory initiatives. For example, the SEC desires to expand its registration and disclosure program to municipal securities and certain financial futures, including GNMA and possibly other interest rate and index forward and futures contracts. We hasten to point out that the ills the disclosure programs are supposed to cure for both kinds of instruments have not worked in the private equity sector, and we see no reason why they should work in the municipal or futures area. The corporate disclosure system did not prevent the equity funding or the Penn Central problems, and no disclosure program that we are aware of would have prevented the New York City bond problems. The cost to municipalities of increased regulatory disclosure cannot be justified as being in the public interest.

The claim by the SEC that they should regulate financial (and other if Congress so desires) futures will place the SEC in a turf battle with the Commodities Futures Trading Commission (CFTC). Although Congress clearly gave the jurisdiction to the CFTC for all futures contracts, the SEC claims that it is better equipped and more experienced to deal with these new and developing marketplaces. In fact the SEC is being pressured by its own regulated exchanges to allow them to move into CFTC areas.

Another area that the SEC seems to be moving into is corporate governance. The chairman of the SEC has said that he believes that the ideal board of directors of a corporation should be composed almost entirely of outside directors, except for the chief executive officer. The thrust of the argument for more outside directors is that corporations should be more responsive to the desires of shareholders and society in general. If the board is a rubber stamp for management, then such a goal cannot be met. To date the SEC has not mandated board composition but has forced corporations to disclose board composition by inside and outside directors, hoping that disclosure will encourage the use of more outside directors.

Corporate spokesmen have objected to any encroachment by the SEC into this area, an area previously left to the private sector to determine. On the other hand, corporations are in fact beginning to place more outsiders on boards as seats become available. Why? Outside directors by their very presence can serve to relieve the social and political pressure on management, they can help take the heat. Outside board members serve as risk-shifting devices or insurance for management. Thus, while some vocal opposition is heard, corporate management basically may not be opposed to the substance of this regulation and may respond themselves to SEC suggestions that more outside directors be appointed. Certainly, taken to the extreme, investors would stand to lose profits if all board members were outsiders, but the optimal number of outsiders appears not to be zero. If outside directors are becoming more popular because they are to the benefit of owners and managers, we must ask whether SEC regulatory action is necessary at all in this area?

We have made a strong case in this book that the regulatory programs that the SEC administers should be judged in terms of their costs and benefits and that many of the SEC's regulations are antiquated in today's trading environment. The much publicized ten-year effort by Harvard Professor Louis Loss to codify the securities laws certainly is not in the spirit of a reexamination of the purposes of the laws. This 900-page (1,500 if you count notes) document, which is now being discussed in congressional and securities law circles, mainly codifies what is in place. The most sweeping of the proposed changes in that document is that issuers would be required to register instead of registering each separate securities issue. Any cost savings from that proposal may be more than wiped out by increased annual reporting requirements. In addition, not to ask whether the rules being codified were doing what they were intended to do, and hence whether they are worth retaining, is distressing if not surprising. Nevertheless, as the public choice theory would predict, even this regulatory effort will have its constituent groups—lawyers and accountants—and also of course opposing groups who pay for these new programs—investors.

Appendix A:
Deregulation Calculations

Trade Sizes, Tables A.1 and A.2

The trade sizes were available for selected years from the NYSE *Public Transaction Studies,* specifically for the years noted:

	Institutions (number of shares)	Individuals (number of shares)
1960	200	93
1961	205	91
1963	256	—
1966	376	—
1969	644	130
1971	713	172
1974	950	216

The years 1960 to 1977 for which no data are available were modeled in the following manner.

For institutions the model used was a curvilinear regression model:

$$\ln (\text{shares/transaction}) = -1.945 + 0.11984 \ (\text{year}),$$

or

$$\text{shares/transaction} = e^{-1.945 + 0.11984(\text{year})}.$$

The relevant statistics were

	R-square	T-values
Unadjusted	0.9859	18.665 (year)
Adjusted	0.9830	−4.558 (constant)

With this model a curvilinear interpolation between the actual data points could be made to estimate the data for the missing years. Where this method was inappropriate, such as the data point for 1969 which is out of line with the rest, a straight-line interpolation was used.

For individuals straight-line interpolation was used between every two actual data points.

Average Share Price, Tables A.3 and A.4

The average share price was determined by using the aggregate data presented in the *Public Transaction Study* (1976, p. 10). The figures for shares traded per day and dollars per day are available for institutions and individuals, from which average share price is determined.

Since the data are intermittent, some method was again needed to estimate the data for the missing years. This was accomplished by first obtaining the overall average share price (of all shares trades) for each year from the NYSE *Fact Book*. Then the missing data were determined by using a weighted volume distribution of institutions and individuals consistent with the overall average share price. For example, for 1970

($39/share) 0.559 + ($25/share) 0.441 = $32.8/share overall,
Institutions   Individuals

where 0.559 and 0.441 are the respective rates of total public volume.

The average value per trade is the average trade size (in shares) multiplied by the average share price.

Effective Transactions Cost, Tables A.5 and A.6

The commission cost for the average trade size was determined, assuming the commission structure for round lots. For example, in 1962 the average value for institutions was $10,992, and the relevant number of shares as 229:

$4,800/100 shares = (4,800 (0.004) + 19) 2.29 = 98.47

$\frac{\$\ 98.47}{\$10,992} = 0.00896$ or 0.896% (effective transaction cost),

where 2.29 is the number of round lots.

For the years 1975, 1976, and 1977 when the rates were negotiable, the effective cost was found in the SEC's *Staff Report on the Securities Industry in 1977* (May 22, 1978).

For 1972 to 1974 when multiple round lot rates were available, the single round lot rate schedule was used to estimate the individuals' effective transactions cost, because this seemed to give a more accurate estimate. Also there is little difference in effective cost regardless of which schedule is used for these trades.

Distribution of Volume over Various Trade Sizes, Tables A.7 to A.10

In the 10,000 and over category, since the aggregate volume (the block trades) is known accurately from 1965 to 1977, these data were used for both individuals and institutions.

Assumption 1. All large block trades are by either institutions or individuals, not the NYSE members.

Assumption 2. For all years about 85 percent of all large block volume is due to institutions, with about 15 percent to individuals. These figures follow from the approximate data for 1977 which originally had 45 percent of all institutional trades in large block and 10 percent of all individual trades in large blocks.

In the 0–199 share category the percentage for the missing years are interpolated on a straight-line basis from 1960 to 1969 and from 1969 to 1977.

In the 200–999 share category the percentages for the missing years are interpolated on a straight-line basis from 1960 to 1969 and from 1969 to 1977.

In the 1,000–9,999 share category the percentages are determined by the percentage calculated for the other three categories:

		Initial observed data		
		0–199	200–999	1,000–9,999	10,000 and over
1960	Institutions	21.4%	46.0%	32.6%	32.6%
	Individuals	55.2%	35.0%	9.7%	9.7%
1969	Institutions	5.5%	17.3%	77.1%	71.1%
	Individuals	41.8%	40.0%	17.2%	17.2%
1977	Institutions	2%	10%	43%	45%
	Individuals	12%	40%	38%	10%

Commissions in Cents per Share, Tables A.11 and A.12

The commissions for any given category of trade size are calculated from an amount of principal which is determined by multiplying the average price per share traded (by individuals or institutions) by the average trade size. For example, in 1974 for individuals the average price per share traded is $23.05. At 600 shares, this would make a trade of six round lots and $13,830. This method will cause some distortion due to the average price per share on very large orders being smaller than the average price per share traded and the inverse being true with very small trades.

These prices per share are based on the approximate price per share data for 1977, extrapolated from 1976 and using the overall average per share traded to check for consistency.

Table A.1 Institutional trade size

Year[a] x	Average trade size[b] y	Slope of y Full year y'	Half year[c]	Average trade size estimate[d]	Averaging to smooth out extreme estimates
1960	200				
1961	205	25.63			
1962	(229)	28.89	27.26	205 + 27.26 = 232.26	229
1963	256	32.57	30.73	256 − 30.73 = 225.27	
1964	(291)	36.71	34.64	256 + 34.64 = 290.64	
1965	(332)	41.39			
1966	376	46.66	44.025	376 − 44.025 = 331.975	
1967	(426)	52.60	49.63	376 + 49.63 = 425.63	
1968	(531)	59.29	55.94	426 + 55.94 = 481.9	(482 + 581)/2
1969	644	66.84	63.065	644 − 63.065 = 580.935	= 531
1970	(679)	75.35	71.095	644 + 71.095 = 715.095	(644 + 713)/2
1971	713	84.95	80.15	713 − 80.15 = 632.85	= 678.5
1972	(790)	95.76			
1973	(870)	107.96			
1974	950	121.70	129.445	950 + 129 = 1,079	
1975	(1,079)	137.19	137.19	1,079 + 137 = 1,216	
1976	(1,216)				
1977	(1,350)[e]				

Note: $y = e^{-1.945 + 0.11984(x)}$, average trade size ($y$) as an exponential function of the year (x), $y' = e^{-1.945 + 0.11984(x)}(0.11984)$, first derivative used to obtain the slope of y, x = year, y = shares/transaction.
[a]The years 1971 to 1974 form a straight line.
[b]Modeled data are given in parentheses.
[c]For example, 61.5 years.
[d]The estimate was either projected forward or backward from an actual data point.
[e]Estimated.

Table A.2 Individual trade size

Year[a]	Average trade size[b]
1960	93
1961	91
1962	(95)
1963	(100)
1964	(105)
1965	(110)
1966	(115)
1967	(120)
1968	(125)
1969	130
1970	(151)
1971	172
1972	(187)
1973	(201)
1974	216
1975	(231)
1976	(245)
1977	(260)

[a]Three straight lines were formed: 1960 to 1968, 1969 to 1971, and 1972 to 1977.
[b]Modeled data are given in parentheses.

Table A.3 Average share price

	Average combined share price	Percent of public volume		Average share price	
		Institutions	Individuals	Institutions	Individuals
1960	39.6			46.35	32.00
1961	40.8			48.95	38.68
1962	39.9			(48.0)	(38.5)
1963	40.6			46.90	38.46
1964	40.8			(46.5)	(36.08)
1965	40.5			46.00	33.70
1966	44.7			45.87	38.20
1967	43.4			(45.65)	(37.00)
1968	44.0			(45.65)	(37.00)
1969	41.3	55.9	44.1	45.45	35.82
1970	32.8	55.9	44.1	(39.00)	(25.00)[a]
1971	35.6	59.7	40.3	40.31	27.94
1972	36.6			(41.5)	(29.00)
1973	34.3			(40.00)	(27.00)
1974	29.5	58.9	41.1	35.69	23.05
1975	27.2			(35.00)	(22.00)
1976	27.2			35.30	20.05

[a]$0.559(39.00) + 25.00(0.441) = 32.8$.

Table A.4 Average value per share traded

	Individuals			Institutions		
	$/day ($1,000)	Shrs/day ($1,000)	$/shr	$/shr	$/day	Shrs/day
1960	$112	3.5	32.00	46.25	74	1.6
1961[a]	147	3.8	38.68	48.95	93	1.9
1962	—	—			—	—
1963[b]	250	6.5	38.46	46.90	136	2.9
1964	—	—			—	—
1965[c]	182	5.4	33.70	46.00	161	3.5
1966[b]	233	6.1	38.20	45.87	211	4.6
1967	—	—			—	—
1968	—	—			—	—
1969[d]	283	7.9	35.82	45.45	459	10.1
1970	—	—			—	—
1971[e]	299	10.7	27.94	40.31	641	15.9
1972	—	—			—	—
1973	—	—			—	—
1974[f]	219	9.5	23.05	35.69	489	13.7
1975	—	—			—	—
1976[f]	377	18.8	20.05	35.30	893	25.3

Source: The New York Stock Exchange, *Public Transaction Study* (New York, 1976), p. 10.
[a]September.
[b]October.
[c]March.
[d]Full year.
[e]First half.
[f]First quarter.

Table A.5 Institutional transactions costs

	Average value/trade	Average volume/trade	Effective cost
1960	$9,250 $4,625/100 shares (4,625(0.005) + 19)2 = 84.25	200 shares	0.00911 = 84.25/9,250
1961	$10,035 $4,895.12/100 shares (4,895(0.005) + 19)2.05 = 89.12	205 shares	0.00888
1962	$10,992 $4,800.00/100 shares (4,800(0.005) + 19)2.29 = 98.47	229 shares	0.00896
1963	$12,006 $4,689.84/100 shares (4,689.85(0.005) + 19)2.56 = 108.67	256 shares	0.00905
1964	$13,532 $4,650.17/100 shares (4,650.17(0.005) + 19)2.91 = 122.95	291 shares	0.00909
1965	$15,272 $4,600/100 shares (4,600(0.005) + 19)3.32 = 139.44	332 shares	0.00913
1966	$17,247 $4,586.97/100 shares (4,586.97(0.005) + 19)3.76 = 157.68	376 shares	0.00914
1967	$19,447 $4,565.02/100 shares (4,565.02(0.005) + 19)4.26 = 178.18	426 shares	0.00916
1968	$24,240 $4,564.97/100 shares (4,564.97(0.005) + 19)5.31 = 222.09	531 shares	0.00916
1969	$29,270 $4,545.03/100 shares (4,545.03(0.005) + 19)6.44 = 268.71	644 shares	0.00918
1970	$26,481 $3,900/100 shares (3,900(0.005) + 19)6.79 = 261.42	679 shares	0.00987
1971	$28,741 $4,031.00/100 shares (4,031.00(0.005) + 19)7.13 = 279.18	713 shares	0.00971
1972	$32,785 32,785(0.004) + 142 + 6(7.9) = 320.54	790 shares	0.00978
1973	$34,800 34,800(0.004) + 142 + 6(8.7) = 333.40	870 shares	0.00958
1974	$33,906 (33,906(0.004) + 142 + 6(9.5))1.15 = 384.82	950 shares	0.01135
1975	$37,765 Negotiable[a]	1,079 shares	0.65%
1976	Negotiable		0.5%
1977	Negotiable		0.45%

[a]Source: SEC Report to Congress on the Effect of the Absence of Fixed Rates of Commission.

Table A.6 Individual transactions costs

	Average value/trade	Average volume/trade	Effective cost
1960	$2,976 $3,200/100 shares $(3,200(0.005) + 19)0.93 = 32.55$	93 shares	0.01094
1961	$3,520 $3,868.13/100 shares $(3,868.13(0.005) + 19)0.91 = 34.89$	91 shares	0.00991
1962	$3,658 $3,850.53/100 shares $(3,850.53(0.005) + 19)1.0 = 36.34$	95 shares	0.00993
1963	$3,846 $3,846/100 shares $(3,846(0.005) + 19)1.0 = 38.23$	100 shares	0.00994
1964	$3,788 $3,607.62/100 shares $(3,607.62(0.005) + 19)1.05 = 38.89$	105 shares	0.01014
1965	$4,070 $3,700/100 shares $(3,700(0.005) + 19)1.1 = 41.25$	110 shares	0.01014
1966	$4,393 $3,820/100 shares $(3,820(0.005) + 19)1.15 = 43.82$	115 shares	0.00997
1967	$4,440 $3,700/100 shares $(3,700(0.005) + 19)1.2 = 45.00$	120 shares	0.01014
1968	$4,625 $3,700/100 shares $(3,700(0.005) + 19)1.25 = 46.88$	125 shares	0.01014
1969	$4,657 $3,582.31/100 shares $(3,582.31(0.005) + 19)1.51 = 47.57$	130 shares	0.01030
1970	$3,775 $2,500.00/100 shares $(2,500(0.005) + 19)1.51 + 15.00 = 62.57$	151 shares	0.01657
1971	$4,806 $2,794.19/100 shares $(2,794.19(0.005) + 19)1.72 + 15.00 = 71.71$	172 shares	0.01492
1972	$5,423 $2,900.00/100 shares $(2,900(0.009) + 22)1.87 = 89.95$	187 shares	0.01659
1973	$5,427 $2,700.00/100 shares $(2,700(0.009) + 22)2.01 = 93.06$	201 shares	0.01715
1974	$4,979 $2,305.09/100 shares $((2,305.09(0.013) + 12)2.16)1.10 = 99.71$	216 shares	0.02003
1975	Negotiable		1.7%
1976	Negotiable		1.55%
1977	Negotiable		1.45%

Table A.7 Distribution of volume over various trade sizes for institutions

	Total volume (in hundreds)[a]	100 shrs (0–199)	600 shrs (200–999)	5,500 shrs (1,000–9,999)	23,000 shrs (10,000 and over)
1960	(0.316) 100% 232,867	21.4% 49,834	46.0% 107,119	28.1% 65,436	4.5% 10,589
1961	(0.338) 100% 338,583	19.6% 66,362	42.8% 144,914	34.6% 117,150	3.0% 10,157
1962	(0.324) 100% 297,930	17.9% 53,329	39.6% 117,980	39.0% 116,193	3.5% 10,428
1963	(0.309) 100% 322,865	16.1% 51,981	36.4% 117,523	43.5% 140,446	4.0% 12,915
1964	(0.351) 100% 408,946	14.3% 58,479	33.2% 135,770	47.5% 194,249	5.0% 20,447
1965	(0.393) 100% 568,152	12.6% 71,587	30.1% 171,014	50.3% 285,780	7.0% 41,023
1966	(0.429) 100% 716,560	10.8% 77,388	26.9% 192,755	52.2% 374,044	10.1% 72,503
1967	(0.467) 100% 1,020,150	9.0% 91,814	23.7% 241,776	53.2% 542,720	14.1% 143,960
1968	(0.506) 100% 1,261,872	7.3% 92,117	20.5% 258,684	52.2% 658,697	19.7% 248,779
1969	(0.544) 100% 1,271,470	5.5% 69,931	17.3% 219,964	50.3% 639,821	26.9% 341,754
1970	(0.552) 100% 1,324,364	5.1% 67,543	16.4% 217,196	49.6% 656,885	28.9% 383,272
1971	(0.597) 100% 1,871,506	4.6% 86,089	15.5% 290,083	48.4% 905,809	31.5% 588,656
1972	(0.594) 100% 1,959,336	4.2% 82,292	14.6% 286,063	47.6% 932,644	33.6% 659,109
1973	(0.582) 100% 1,902,262	3.8% 72,286	13.7% 260,610	49.9% 949,229	32.6% 620,366
1974	(0.589) 100% 1,632,984	3.3% 53,888	12.7% 207,389	55.1% 899,774	28.9% 472,473
1975	(0.581) 100% 2,156,567	2.9% 62,540	11.8% 254,475	54.3% 1,171,016	31.0% 669,544
1976	(0.573) 100% 2,455,822	2.4% 58,940	10.9% 267,685	51.6% 1,267,204	35.1% 861,073
1977	(0.573) 100% 2,412,608	2% 48,252	10% 241,261	45.8% 1,104,975	42.2% 1,018,175

[a]Institutional volume/public volume.

Table A.8 Distribution of volume over various trade sizes for individuals

	Total volume[a]	100 shrs (0–199)	600 shrs (200–999)	5,500 shrs (1,000–9,999)	23,000 shrs (10,000 and over)
1960	(0.684) 100% 504,066	55.2% 278,244	35% 176,423	9.3% 46,878	0.4% 1,869
1961	(0.662) 100% 664,242	53.7% 356,698	35.7% 237,134	10.1% 67,088	0.5% 3,321
1962	(0.676) 100% 621,608	52.2% 324,479	36.3% 225,644	11.0% 68,377	0.5% 3,108
1963	(0.691) 100% 721,381	50.7% 365,740	37.0% 266,911	11.7% 84,402	0.6% 4,328
1964	(0.649) 100% 756,142	49.2% 372,022	37.7% 285,066	12.4% 93,762	0.7% 5,293
1965	(0.607) 100% 877,559	47.8% 419,473	38.3% 336,105	13.1% 114,960	0.8% 7,239
1966	(0.571) 100% 952,474	46.3% 440,995	39.0% 371,465	13.4% 127,632	1.3% 12,795
1967	(0.533) 100% 1,164,325	44.8% 521,618	39.7% 462,237	13.3% 154,855	2.2% 25,405
1968	(0.494) 100% 1,231,946	43.3% 533,433	40.3% 496,474	12.8% 157,689	3.6% 43,902
1969	(0.456) 100% 1,067,292	41.8% 446,128	41.0% 437,590	11.5% 123,264	5.7% 60,310
1970	(0.448) 100% 1,074,484	38.1% 409,378	41.0% 440,538	14.6% 156,875	6.3% 67,636
1971	(0.403) 100% 1,261,322	34.3% 432,633	41.0% 517,142	16.5% 208,118	8.2% 103,880
1972	(0.406) 100% 1,339,210	30.6% 409,798	40.5% 542,380	20.9% 279,895	8.0% 107,297
1973	(0.408) 100% 1,311,018	26.9% 352,664	40.5% 530,962	24.9% 326,443	7.7% 100,990
1974	(0.411) 100% 1,138,695	23.2% 264,177	40.5% 461,171	29.5% 335,915	6.8% 76,914
1975	(0.419) 100% 1,555,253	19.5% 303,274	40.0% 622,101	33.5% 521,010	7.0% 108,996
1976	(0.427) 100% 1,832,208	15.7% 287,657	40.0% 732,883	36.6% 670,588	7.7% 140,176
1977	(0.427) 100% 1,797,877	12% 215,745	40% 719,151	38.8% 697,576	9.2% 165,749

[a]Individual volume/public volume.

Table A.9 Distribution of total public volume (actual data) over various trade size categories (in hundreds)

	0–199	200–999	1,000–9,999	10,000 and over[c]	Total public volume
1960	44.52%	38.48%	15.31%	1.69%[d]	100%
	328,078	283,542	112,824	12,458	736,933
1961				—	100%
				17,400[e]	1,002,825
1962				—	100%
				12,600[e]	919,538
1963				—	100%
				18,500[e]	1,044,246
1964				—	100%
				17,200[e]	1,165,088
1965				3.34%	100%
				48,262	1,445,711
1966				5.11%	100%
				85,798	1,669,034
1967				7.75%	100%
				169,365	2,184,475
1968				11.74%	100%
				292,681	2,493,817
1969[a]	22.07%	28.12%	32.62%	17.19%	100%
	516,059	657,554	762,904	402,064	2,338,762
1970				—	100%
				450,908	2,398,848
1971				—	100%
				692,536	3,132,828
1972				—	100%
				766,406	3,298,546
1973				—	100%
				721,356	3,213,280
1974[b]	13.8%	35%	36.2%	19.82%	100%
	404,273	1,281,490	1,325,427	544,387	2,771,680
1975[b]	11.2%	32.3%	40.4%	20.97%	100%
	542,013	1,563,126	1,955,118	778,540	3,711,820
1976[f]	9.96%	29.5%	42.5%	23.35%	100%
	549,887			1,001,254	4,288,030
1977		30.6%		28.12%	100%
				1,183,424	4,210,485

[a]Source: 1969 NYSE *Public Transaction Study*.
[b]Source: 1974 NYSE *Public Transaction Study*.
[c]Assumed that all large blocks are public trades.
[d]Estimated.
[e]See 1966 NYSE *Fact Book*, p. 20.
[f]Data incomplete if estimates made.

Table A.10 Distribution of public volume between individuals and institutions (in hundreds)

	Total volume				Public volume		
	Total volume	NYSE members	Public individuals	Institutions	Public volume	Individuals	Institutions
1960	100% 958,300	23.1% 221,367	52.6% 504,066	24.3% 232,867	(0.769)[a] 100% 736,933	68.4% 504,066	31.6% 232,867
1961	100% 1,292,300	22.4% 289,475	51.4% 664,242	26.2% 338,583	(0.776) 100% 1,002,825	66.2% 664,242	33.8% 338,583
1962	100% 1,186,500				(0.775)[b] 100%[b] 919,538[b]	67.6%[b] 621,608[b]	32.4%[b] 297,930[b]
1963	100% 1,350,900	22.7% 306,654	53.4% 721,381	23.9% 322,865	(0.773) 100% 1,044,246	69.1% 721,381	30.9% 322,865
1964	100% 1,482,300				(0.786)[b] 100%[b] 1,165,088[b]	64.9%[b] 756,142[b]	35.1%[b] 408,946[b]
1965	100% 1,809,400	20.1% 363,689	48.5% 877,559	31.4% 568,152	(0.799) 100% 1,445,711	60.7% 877,559	39.3% 568,152
1966	100% 2,204,800	24.3% 535,766	43.2% 952,474	32.5% 716,560	(0.757) 100% 1,669,034	57.1% 952,474	42.9% 716,560
1967	100% 2,885,700				(0.757)[b] 100%[b] 2,184,475[b]	53.3%[b] 1,164,325[b]	46.7%[b] 1,020,150[b]
1968	100% 3,298,700				(0.756)[b] 100%[b] 2,493,817[b]	49.4%[b] 1,231,946[b]	50.6%[b] 1,261,872[b]
1969	100% 3,093,600	24.4% 754,838	34.5% 1,067,292	41.1% 1,271,470	(0.756) 100% 2,338,762	45.6% 1,067,292	54.4% 1,271,470
1970	100% 3,123,500	24.2% 755,887	34.4% 1,074,484	42.4% 1,324,364	(0.768) 100% 2,398,848	44.8% 1,074,484	55.2% 1,324,364
1971	100% 4,095,200	23.5% 962,372	30.8% 1,261,322	45.7% 1,871,506	(0.765)[a] 100% 3,132,828	40.3% 1,261,322	59.7% 1,871,506

Table A.10 (continued)

	Total volume		NYSE members	Public individuals	Institutions	Public volume			Individuals	Institutions
	Total volume					Public volume			Individuals	Institutions
1972	100%	4,328,800				$(0.762)^b$	$100\%^b$	$3,298,546^b$	$40.6\%^b$ $1,339,210^b$	$59.4\%^b$ $1,959,336^b$
1973	100%	4,228,000				$(0.760)^b$	$100\%^b$	$3,213,280^b$	$40.8\%^b$ $1,311,018^b$	$59.2\%^b$ $1,902,262^b$
1974	100%	3,661,400	24.3% 889,720	31.1% 1,138,695	44.6% 1,632,984	(0.757)	100%	2,771,680	41.1% 1,138,695	58.9% 1,632,984
1975	100%	4,839,400				$(0.767)^b$	$100\%^b$	$3,711,820^b$	$41.9\%^b$ $1,555,253^b$	$58.1\%^b$ $2,156,567^b$
1976	100%	5,518,700	22.3% 1,230,670	33.2% 1,832,208	44.5% 2,455,822	(0.777)	100%	4,288,030	42.7% 1,832,208	57.3% 2,455,822
1977	100%	5,418,900				$(0.777)^b$	$100\%^b$	$4,210,485^b$	$42.7\%^b$ $1,797,877^b$	$57.3\%^b$ $2,412,608^b$

[a] Public volume/total volume.
[b] Modeled data.

Table A.11
a. Commissions in cents per share based on the average price per share traded by institutions and individuals in each year of a rate change

Trade size	Individuals $\bar{x} \sim \$19.00$/share	Institutions $\bar{x} \sim \$34.50$/share
1977		
100 shares (0–199)	51 cents/share	43 cents/share
600 shares (200–999)	32 cents/share	27 cents/share
5,500 shares (1,000–9,999)	17 cents/share	15 cents/share
23,000 shares (10,000 or more)	6 cents/share	9 cents/share
1974 (September 25, 1973, schedule)		
100 shares	46 cents/share	62 cents/share
600 shares	30 cents/share	41 cents/share
5,500 shares	16 cents/share	21 cents/share
23,000 shares	No data found	No data found
1972 (May 24, 1972, schedule)		
100 shares	48 cents/share	59 cents/share
600 shares	36 cents/share	45 cents/share
5,500 shares	19 cents/share	24 cents/share
23,000 shares	No data found	No data found
1969 (December 5, 1968, schedule)		
100 shares	37 cents/share	42 cents/share
600 shares	37 cents/share	42 cents/share
5,500 shares	21 cents/share	21 cents/share
23,000 shares	21 cents/share	21 cents/share
1960 (March 30, 1959, schedule)		
100 shares	35 cents/share	42 cents/share
600 shares	35 cents/share	42 cents/share
5,500 shares	35 cents/share	42 cents/share
23,000 shares	35 cents/share	42 cents/share

Table A.11 (continued)
b. Detail of calculations

	Individuals	Institutions
1969		
Average trade size	130 shares	644 shares
Average price per share	$35.82	$45.45
100 shares	$3,582 (3,582(0.005) + 19) = $36.91 36.91 cents/share	$4,545 (4,545(0.005) + 19) = $41.725 41.73 cents/share
600 shares	$21,492 (3,582(0.005) + 19)6 = $221.46 36.91 cents/share	$27,270 (4,545(0.005) + 19)6 = $250.35 41.73 cents/share
5,500 shares	$197,010 (3,582(0.005) + 3)55 = $1,150.05 20.91 cents/share	$249,975 (4,545(0.005) + 3)55 = $1,414.875 25.725 cents/share
23,000 shares	$823,560 (3,582(0.005) + 3)230 = $4,809.30 20.91 cents/share	$1,045,350 (4,545(0.005) + 3)230 = $5,916.75 25.725 cents/share
1960		
Average trade size	93 shares	200 shares
Average price per share	$32.00	$46.25
100 shares (applies to all trade sizes)	$3,200 3,200(0.005) + 19 = $35 35 cents/share	$4,625 4,625(0.005) + 19 = $42.125 42 cents/share
1974		
Average trade size	216 shares	950 shares
Average price per share	$23.05	$35.69
100 shares	$2,305 (2,305(0.012) + 12)1.1 = $46.16 46.16 cents/share	$3,569 (3,569(0.009) + 22)1.15 = $62.24 62.24 cents/share
600 shares	$13,830 ((13,830(.009) + 22) + 6(6)) = $182.47 30.41 cents/share	$21,414 21,414(.006) + 82 + 6(6) = $246.48 41.08 cents/share
5,500 shares	$126,775 126,775(0.004) + 142 + 6(10) + 45(4) = $889.10 16.17 cents/share	$196,295 196,295(0.004) + 142 + 6(10) + 45(4) = $1,167.18 21.22 cents/share
23,000 shares	Negotiable	Negotiable

Table A.11 (continued)

	Individuals	Institutions
1972		
Average trade size	187 shares	790 shares
Average price per share	$29.00	$41.50
100 shares	$2,900 2,900(0.009) + 22 = $48.10 48.0 cents/share	$4,150 (4,150(0.009) + 22 = $59.35 59.35 cents/share
600 shares	$17,400 17,400(0.009) + 22 + 6(6) = $214.60 35.77 cents/share	$24,900 24,900(0.006) + 82 + 6(6) = $267.40 44.57 cents/share
5,500 shares	$159,500 159,500(0.004) + 142 + 6(10) + 45(4) = $1,020 18.55 cents/share	$228,250 228,250(0.004) + 142 + 6(10) + 45(4) = $1,295 23.55 cents/share
23,000 shares	Negotiable	Negotiable

Table A.12 Commissions in cents per share based on $35 per share for institutions and $20 per share for individuals

Trade size	Individuals	Institutions
1960–1968 (March 30, 1959, schedule)		
100 shares (0–199)	27 cents/share	36.5 cents/share
600 shares (200–999)	27 cents/share	36.5 cents/share
5,500 shares (1,000–9,999)	27 cents/share	36.5 cents/share
23,000 shares (10,000 or more)	27 cents/share	36.5 cents/share
1969 (December 5, 1969, schedule)		
100 shares	27 cents/share	36.5 cents/share
600 shares	27 cents/share	36.5 cents/share
5,500 shares	14 cents/share	20.5 cents/share
23,000 shares	14 cents/share	20.5 cents/share
1970–1971		
100 shares	40.5 cents/share	51.5 cents/share
600 shares	29.5 cents/share	39.0 cents/share
5,500 shares	14.0 cents/share	14.0 cents/share
23,000 shares	14.0 cents/share	14.0 cents/share

Table A.12 (continued)

Trade size	Individuals	Institutions
1972–1973 (May 24, 1972, schedule)		
100 shares	38 cents/share	54 cents/share
600 shares	28 cents/share	41 cents/share
5,500 shares	15 cents/share	21 cents/share
23,000 shares	8 cents/share[a]	14 cents/share[a]
1974 (September 25, 1973, schedule)		
100 shares	42 cents/share	59 cents/share
600 shares	32 cents/share	47 cents/share
5,500 shares	17 cents/share	24 cents/share
23,000 shares	9 cents/share[a]	15 cents/share[a]
1975 (competitive rates since April 1975)		
100 shares	51 cents/share	54 cents/share
600 shares	32 cents/share	37 cents/share
5,500 shares	18 cents/share	22 cents/share
23,000 shares	6 cents/share	12 cents/share
1976		
100 shares	52 cents/share	49 cents/share
600 shares	32 cents/share	37 cents/share
5,500 shares	18 cents/share	19 cents/share
23,000 shares	7 cents/share	11 cents/share
1977 (negotiable rates)		
100 shares	51 cents/share	43 cents/share
600 shares	32 cents/share	27 cents/share
5,500 shares	18 cents/share	22 cents/share
23,000 shares	6 cents/share	12 cents/share

[a]Estimated.

Table A.13 Documentation for table A.12 using 1977 prices per share throughout: institutions $35 per share, individuals $20 per share

	Individuals	Institutions
1974		
100	$2,000 1.1(2,000(0.013) + 12) = $41.80 41.8 cents/share	$3,500 1.1(3,500(0.009) + 22) = $58.85 58.85 cents/share
600	$12,000 1.15(12,000(0.009) + 22 + 6(6)) = $190.90 31.82 cents/share	$21,000 (21,000(0.006) + 82 + 6(6))1.15 = $280.60 46.77 cents/share
5,500	$110,000 1.15(110,000(0.004) + 142 + 10(6) + 4(45)) = $945.30 17.19 cents/share	$192,500 (192,500(0.004) + 142 + 10(6) + 4(45))1.15 = $1,324.80 24.09 cents/share
23,000	Negotiable, no data found	Negotiable, no data found
1972		
100	$2,000 2,000(0.013) + 12 = $38.00 38 cents/share	$3,500 3,500(0.009) + 22 = $53.50 53.5 cents/share
600	$12,000 12,000(0.009) + 22 + 6(6) = $166 27.67 cents/share	$21,000 21,000(0.006) + 82 + 6(6) = $244 40.67 cents/share
5,500	$110,000 110,000(0.004) + 142 + 10(6) + 4(45) = $822 14.95 cents/share	$192,500 (192,500(0.004) + 142 + 10(6) + 4(45) = $1,152 20.95 cents/share
23,000	Negotiable	Negotiable
1969		
100	$2,000 (2,000)(0.01) + 7 = $27 27 cents/share + $13.5 = 40.5 (1970–71)	$3,500 3,500(0.005) + 19 = $36.50 36.5 cents/share + $15 = $51.5 (1970–71)
600	$12,000 (2,000(0.01) + 7)6 = $162 27 cents/share + $15 = $177 29.5 cents/share (1970–71)	$21,000 (3,500(0.005) + 19)6 = $219 36.5 cents/share + $15 = $234 39.0 cents/share (1970–71)
5,500	$110,000 (2,000(0.005) + 4)55 = $770 14 cents/share	$192,500 (3,500(0.005) + 3)55 = $1,127.50 20.5 cents/share
23,000	$460,000 (2,000(0.005) + 4)230 = $3,220 14 cents/share	$805,000 20.5 cents/share

Table A.13 (continued)

	Individuals	Institutions
1960		
100	$2,000 27 cents/share	$3,500 36.5 cents/share
600	$12,000 27 cents/share	$21,000 36.5 cents/share
5,500	$110,000 27 cents/share	$192,500 36.5 cents/share
23,000	$460,000 27 cents/share	$805,000 36.5 cents/share

Appendix B:
Yearly Changes in Exchange Seat Prices

Table B.1 Percentage of New York Stock Exchange seat price changes for all yearly holding periods from 1929 to 1978

End year	Beginning year									
	1929	1930	1931	1932	1933	1934	1935	1936	1937	1938
1929	−27.0									
1930	−41.0	−52.4								
1931	−38.8	−43.9	−34.0							
1932	−34.9	−37.4	−28.2	−22.0						
1933	−26.3	−26.1	−14.5	−2.7	21.4					
1934	−25.9	−25.7	−17.0	−10.4	−4.0	−24.0				
1935	−17.9	−16.2	−6.2	2.4	12.1	7.7	52.6			
1936	−17.0	−15.5	−7.0	−0.5	5.8	1.1	16.5	−11.0		
1937	−20.3	−19.4	−13.1	−9.0	−6.1	−12.0	−7.6	−28.1	−41.9	
1938	−19.0	−18.1	−12.3	−8.7	−6.2	−11.0	−7.4	−21.6	−26.3	−6.7
1939	−18.3	−17.4	−12.2	−9.0	−7.0	−11.0	−8.2	−19.1	−21.7	−9.1
1940	−21.4	−20.9	−16.7	−14.6	−13.6	−17.7	−16.6	−26.1	−29.4	−24.7
1941	−21.4	−21.0	−17.2	−15.3	−14.6	−18.2	−17.4	−25.4	−28.0	−24.0
1942	−19.4	−18.8	−15.1	−13.1	−12.2	−15.3	−14.2	−20.9	−22.5	−17.9
1943	−15.4	−14.5	−10.5	−8.2	−6.9	−9.3	−7.5	−13.1	−13.4	−7.5
1944	−12.7	−11.7	−7.7	−5.3	−3.8	−5.8	−3.7	−8.5	−8.2	−2.0
1945	−10.1	−8.9	−4.8	−2.3	−0.6	−2.3	−0	−4.1	−3.3	3.0
1946	−11.0	−10.0	−6.4	−4.1	−2.7	−4.4	−2.5	−6.4	−5.9	−0.8
1947	−11.1	−10.2	−6.7	−4.7	−3.4	−5.0	−3.4	−7.0	−6.6	−2.0
1948	−12.3	−11.4	−8.3	−6.5	−5.5	−7.0	−5.7	−9.1	−8.9	−5.1
1949	−11.2	−10.3	−7.2	−5.5	−4.4	−5.8	−4.5	−7.6	−7.3	−3.6
1950	−10.3	−9.5	−6.5	−4.8	−3.7	−5.0	−3.7	−6.6	−6.3	−2.8
1951	−9.8	−8.9	−6.0	−4.4	−3.3	−4.6	−3.3	−6.0	−5.6	−2.3
1952	−9.6	−8.8	−6.0	−4.4	−3.5	−4.6	−3.4	−6.0	−5.6	−2.5
1953	−9.6	−8.8	−6.2	−4.7	−3.8	−4.9	−3.7	−6.2	−5.9	−3.0
1954	−6.9	−6.0	−3.3	−1.7	−0.6	−1.6	−0.3	−2.5	−2.0	1.1
1955	−6.7	−5.8	−3.2	−1.6	−0.6	−1.5	−0.3	−2.4	−1.9	1.0
1956	−6.6	−5.7	−3.2	−1.7	−0.8	−1.7	−0.5	−2.5	−2.1	0.7
1957	−7.0	−6.2	−3.8	−2.4	−1.5	−2.4	−1.3	−3.3	−2.9	−0.3
1958	−4.6	−3.7	−1.3	0.2	1.2	0.4	1.6	−0.2	0.3	3.0
1959	−4.0	−3.2	−0.8	0.7	1.6	1.0	2.1	0.4	0.9	3.5
1960	−4.1	−3.3	−1.0	0.4	1.4	0.7	1.8	0.1	0.6	3.1
1961	−3.0	−2.1	0.2	1.6	2.5	1.9	3.0	1.4	2.0	4.4
1962	−3.3	−2.5	−0.2	1.1	2.0	1.4	2.4	1.0	1.4	3.7
1963	−2.9	−2.1	0.1	1.4	2.2	1.7	2.7	1.2	1.7	3.9
1964	−2.8	−2.0	0.1	1.3	2.2	1.6	2.6	1.2	1.7	3.8
1965	−2.4	−1.7	0.4	1.6	2.5	1.9	2.9	1.5	2.0	4.1
1966	−2.5	−1.7	0.3	1.5	2.3	1.7	2.7	1.4	1.8	3.8
1967	−0.6	0.2	2.2	3.5	4.3	3.8	4.8	3.6	4.1	6.2
1968	−0.3	0.5	2.5	3.7	4.6	4.1	5.1	3.9	4.4	6.4
1969	−1.4	−0.7	1.2	2.4	3.1	2.6	3.5	2.4	2.8	4.6
1970	−2.8	−2.1	−0.3	0.7	1.4	0.9	1.7	0.5	0.9	2.6
1971	−2.4	−1.8	−0	1.0	1.7	1.2	2.0	0.9	1.3	2.9
1972	−2.6	−2.0	−0.3	0.8	1.4	0.9	1.7	0.6	0.9	2.5

Table B.1 (continued)

End year	Beginning year									
	1929	1930	1931	1932	1933	1934	1935	1936	1937	1938
1973	-3.6	-3.0	-1.4	-0.4	0.2	-0.3	0.4	-0.7	-0.4	1.1
1974	-4.3	-3.8	-2.2	-1.3	-0.8	-1.2	-0.6	-1.7	-1.4	-0
1975	-4.9	-4.3	-2.8	-2.0	-1.4	-1.9	-1.3	-2.4	-2.2	-0.1
1976	-4.0	-3.5	-2.0	-1.1	-0.6	-1.0	-0.4	-1.4	-1.2	0.2
1977	-5.1	-4.5	-3.1	-2.3	-1.8	-2.3	-1.7	-2.7	-2.5	-1.3
1978	-4.0	-3.5	-2.0	-1.2	-0.7	-1.1	-0.5	-1.5	-1.3	-0

End year	Beginning year									
	1939	1940	1941	1942	1943	1944	1945	1946	1947	1948
1939	-11.4									
1940	-32.4	-48.4								
1941	-29.1	-36.5	-21.9							
1942	-20.5	-23.3	-6.5	12.0						
1943	-7.7	-6.7	13.7	37.1	67.9					
1944	-1.2	0.9	19.4	37.5	52.4	38.3				
1945	4.5	7.4	24.3	39.6	50.3	42.2	46.2			
1946	-0	1.7	13.9	22.9	25.7	14.2	3.8	-26.3		
1947	-1.5	-0.2	9.7	16.0	16.9	6.7	-2.1	-19.9	-12.9	
1948	-5.0	-4.2	3.5	7.7	7.0	-2.2	-10.3	-23.8	-22.5	-31.1
1949	-3.4	-2.5	4.6	8.5	8.0	3.5	-5.9	-15.7	-11.8	-11.3
1950	-2.4	-1.6	5.0	8.5	8.0	1.5	-3.7	-11.4	-7.2	-5.2
1951	-2.0	-1.1	4.9	8.0	7.6	1.8	-2.6	-9.0	-5.1	-3.0
1952	-2.2	-1.5	4.0	6.7	6.2	0.9	-3.0	-8.5	-5.1	-3.5
1953	-2.8	-2.1	2.8	5.2	4.6	-0.2	-3.8	-8.7	-5.8	-4.6
1954	1.6	2.5	7.7	10.4	10.2	6.1	3.3	-0.6	3.2	5.7
1955	1.4	2.3	7.1	9.5	9.3	5.5	2.9	-0.7	2.7	4.8
1956	1.1	1.9	6.3	8.5	8.3	4.7	2.3	-1.0	2.0	3.8
1957	-0	0.7	4.7	6.6	6.3	2.9	0.6	-2.5	-0	1.4
1958	3.5	4.3	8.5	10.6	10.5	7.5	5.6	3.0	5.9	7.8
1959	4.0	4.9	8.8	10.9	10.8	8.0	6.2	3.8	6.6	8.4
1960	3.5	4.3	8.0	9.9	9.8	7.1	5.4	3.1	5.6	7.2
1961	4.9	5.7	9.4	11.2	11.2	8.7	7.1	5.1	7.6	9.2
1962	4.1	4.9	8.3	10.0	9.9	7.5	6.0	4.0	6.3	7.7
1963	4.4	5.1	8.4	10.0	9.9	7.6	6.2	4.4	6.5	7.9
1964	4.2	4.9	8.0	9.6	9.5	7.3	5.9	4.1	6.2	7.4
1965	4.5	5.2	8.2	9.7	9.6	7.5	6.2	4.5	6.5	7.7
1966	4.2	4.8	7.7	9.1	9.0	6.9	5.7	4.1	5.9	7.0
1967	6.6	7.3	10.3	11.8	11.8	9.9	8.8	7.3	9.3	10.5
1968	6.9	7.6	10.4	11.9	11.9	10.0	9.0	7.6	9.5	10.7
1969	5.0	5.6	8.3	9.5	9.4	7.7	6.6	5.2	6.8	7.8
1970	2.9	3.4	5.8	6.9	6.8	5.0	3.9	2.5	3.9	4.7
1971	3.2	3.7	6.1	7.2	7.0	5.3	4.3	2.9	4.3	5.1
1972	2.8	3.3	5.5	6.6	6.4	4.7	3.7	2.4	3.7	4.4
1973	1.3	1.7	3.8	4.7	4.5	2.9	1.8	0.5	1.7	2.3
1974	0.2	0.5	2.5	3.4	3.1	1.5	0.5	-0.8	0.2	0.8
1975	-0.7	-0.3	1.6	2.3	2.1	0.5	-0.5	-1.8	-0.8	-0.4
1976	0.4	0.7	2.6	3.4	3.1	1.6	0.7	-.6	0.4	0.9
1977	-1.1	-0.8	0.9	1.6	1.4	-0.1	-1.2	-2.3	-1.4	-1.0
1978	0.2	0.5	2.3	3.0	2.8	1.3	0.4	-0.7	0.2	0.7

Table B.1 (continued)

End year	Beginning year									
	1949	1950	1951	1952	1953	1954	1955	1956	1957	1958
1949	14.3									
1950	11.3	8.3								
1951	8.7	6.1	3.8							
1952	5.0	2.0	−1.0	−5.6						
1953	1.8	−1.1	−4.0	−7.7	−9.8					
1954	13.5	13.4	14.7	18.6	32.8	95.7				
1955	11.3	10.8	11.3	13.3	20.4	39.1	−1.1			
1956	9.2	8.5	8.5	9.5	13.6	22.7	−2.8	−4.5		
1957	5.8	4.8	4.3	4.4	6.5	11.1	−8.0	−11.3	−17.6	
1958	12.7	12.5	13.1	14.5	18.2	24.8	11.5	16.0	27.9	98.6
1959	12.9	12.8	13.3	14.5	17.7	23.1	12.2	15.8	23.5	51.2
1960	11.2	10.9	11.2	12.0	14.4	18.4	8.9	11.0	15.3	28.2
1961	13.2	13.1	13.5	14.5	17.0	20.9	12.9	15.4	19.8	31.6
1962	11.2	10.9	11.2	11.8	13.8	16.7	9.4	11.0	13.8	21.4
1963	11.1	10.9	11.1	11.8	13.5	16.1	9.6	11.0	13.4	19.6
1964	10.4	10.2	10.3	10.8	12.3	14.6	8.6	9.7	11.6	16.6
1965	10.5	10.3	10.4	10.9	12.3	14.4	8.9	10.0	11.7	16.0
1966	9.6	9.4	9.4	9.8	11.0	12.8	7.7	8.6	10.0	13.6
1967	13.3	13.2	13.5	14.2	15.6	17.7	13.2	14.5	16.4	20.5
1968	13.4	13.3	13.6	14.2	15.5	17.5	13.2	14.5	16.2	19.9
1969	10.2	9.9	10.0	10.4	11.4	12.9	8.8	9.6	10.7	13.5
1970	6.7	6.4	6.3	6.3	7.1	8.2	4.2	4.6	5.3	7.3
1971	7.0	6.7	6.6	6.8	7.5	8.5	4.8	5.2	5.9	7.8
1972	6.3	5.9	5.8	5.9	6.5	7.4	3.9	4.2	4.8	6.5
1973	3.9	3.5	3.3	3.3	3.7	4.5	1.1	1.2	1.5	2.9
1974	2.3	1.8	1.5	1.4	1.8	2.4	−0.9	−0.9	−0.7	0.4
1975	1.0	0.5	0.2	0.1	0.3	0.8	−2.3	−2.4	−2.3	−1.3
1976	2.3	1.9	1.7	1.6	1.9	2.4	−0.5	−0.5	−0.3	0.7
1977	0.2	−0.2	−0.5	−0.7	−0.5	−0.1	−3.0	−3.1	−3.0	−2.2
1978	2.0	1.6	1.3	1.2	1.5	2.0	−0.8	−0.7	−0.6	0.3

Table B.1 (continued)

End year	Beginning year									
	1959	1960	1961	1962	1963	1964	1965	1966	1967	1968
1959	15.1									
1960	3.9	−6.3								
1961	14.7	14.6	40.0							
1962	7.4	5.0	11.1	−11.9						
1963	8.1	6.4	11.0	−1.2	10.8					
1964	6.7	5.1	8.1	−0.8	5.3	−0				
1965	7.5	6.2	8.9	2.3	7.5	5.9	12.2			
1966	5.9	4.7	6.6	0.9	4.4	2.4	3.6	−4.3		
1967	13.9	13.8	17.0	13.5	19.5	2.2	3.0	39.9	104.5	
1968	14.0	13.9	16.7	13.7	18.6	20.2	25.9	30.8	53.0	14.4
1969	7.9	7.2	8.8	5.4	8.1	7.7	9.3	8.6	13.3	−5.7
1970	1.9	0.8	1.6	−2.0	−0.7	−2.2	−2.6	−5.3	−5.6	−27.0
1971	2.8	1.9	2.6	−0.5	0.9	−0.3	−0.4	−2.3	−1.9	−18.4
1972	1.9	0.9	1.5	−1.4	−0.3	−1.4	−1.6	−3.4	−3.3	−16.7
1973	−1.5	−2.6	−2.4	−5.2	−4.6	−6.0	−6.7	−8.8	−9.4	−20.9
1974	−3.8	−4.9	−4.8	−7.6	−7.2	−8.7	−9.6	−11.7	−12.6	−22.6
1975	−5.3	−6.5	−6.5	−9.1	−8.9	−10.4	−11.3	−13.3	−14.3	−23.1
1976	−3.0	−4.0	−3.9	−6.2	−5.8	−7.0	−7.5	−9.2	−9.6	−17.5
1977	−5.8	−6.8	−6.8	−9.2	−9.0	−10.3	−11.0	−12.7	−13.4	−20.6
1978	−3.0	−3.9	−3.8	−5.9	−5.5	−6.5	−6.9	−8.3	−8.6	−15.3

End year	Beginning year									
	1969	1970	1971	1972	1973	1974	1975	1976	1977	1978
1969	−37.9									
1970	−41.7	−45.3								
1971	−27.0	−20.9	14.3							
1972	−23.1	−17.5	1.4	−10.0						
1973	−26.6	−23.4	−14.3	−25.8	−38.9					
1974	−27.5	−25.2	−19.1	−27.9	−35.4	−31.8				
1975	−27.4	−25.4	−20.7	−27.6	−32.6	−29.3	−26.7			
1976	−20.8	−18.0	−12.2	−16.7	−18.4	−10.1	3.3	45.5		
1977	−23.7	−21.7	−17.6	−22.0	−24.2	−20.0	−15.7	−9.5	−43.7	
1978	−17.5	−14.9	−10.1	−13.1	−13.6	−7.4	−0	10.9	−3.2	66.7

Table B.2 Percentage of Philadelphia Stock Exchange seat price changes for all yearly holding periods from 1929 to 1978

End year	Beginning year									
	1929	1930	1931	1932	1933	1934	1935	1936	1937	1938
1929	−8.8									
1930	−29.3	−45.2								
1931	−53.6	−66.9	−80.0							
1932	−51.6	−60.8	−66.8	−45.0						
1933	−35.4	−40.7	−39.2	6.1	104.5					
1934	−39.3	−44.1	−43.8	−20.6	−4.7	−55.6				
1935	−35.3	−38.9	−37.6	−17.0	−4.8	−35.0	−5.0			
1936	−23.9	−25.8	−22.0	2.4	19.6	−0	50.0	136.8		
1937	−33.6	−36.2	−34.8	−20.6	−14.6	−13.3	−20.6	−27.5	−77.8	
1938	−31.0	−33.1	−31.4	−18.3	−12.7	−26.4	−16.4	−19.9	−53.5	−2.5
1939	−30.3	−32.2	−30.6	−18.9	−14.3	−25.8	−17.8	−20.7	−45.0	−13.4
1940	−31.2	−32.9	−31.6	−21.6	−18.0	−28.0	−22.0	−25.0	−43.8	−23.3
1941	−33.5	−35.2	−34.2	−25.9	−23.4	−32.2	−28.0	−31.3	−46.4	−33.1
1942	−34.8	−36.5	−35.7	−28.5	−26.6	−34.5	−31.2	−34.3	−47.0	−36.9
1943	−29.8	−31.1	−29.8	−22.1	−19.6	−26.8	−22.6	−24.5	−35.9	−23.5
1944	−28.2	−29.3	−28.0	−20.6	−18.1	−24.7	−20.6	−22.1	−32.2	−20.5
1945	−17.9	−18.4	−16.2	−7.2	−3.4	−9.3	−3.2	−3.0	−12.2	4.3
1946	−15.3	−15.7	−13.4	−4.5	−0.7,	−6.0	−0	0.5	−7.8	8.0
1947	−18.1	−18.6	−16.7	−8.9	−5.8	−10.9	−6.0	−6.0	−13.6	−1.0
1948	−18.6	−19.1	−17.3	−10.1	−7.3	−12.1	−7.7	−7.9	−14.9	−3.8
1949	−21.5	−22.1	−20.6	−14.3	−12.0	−16.5	−12.9	−13.5	−19.9	−10.9
1950	−18.1	−18.5	−16.8	−10.4	−7.9	−12.1	−8.3	−8.5	−14.5	−5.2
1951	−16.4	−16.7	−15.1	−8.7	−6.2	−10.2	−6.4	−6.5	−12.1	−3.0
1952	−18.2	−18.6	−17.1	−11.3	−9.1	−12.9	−9.6	−9.9	−15.1	−7.2
1953	−16.1	−16.4	−14.8	−9.0	−6.8	−10.4	−7.0	−7.1	−12.1	−4.2
1954	−12.9	−13.1	−11.4	−5.5	−3.1	−6.5	−2.9	−2.8	−7.5	0.6
1955	−11.5	−11.6	−9.8	−4.0	−1.6	−4.9	−1.4	−1.2	−5.6	2.3
1956	−11.6	−11.7	−10.1	−4.5	−2.3	−5.4	−2.1	−2.0	−6.2	1.2
1957	−9.8	−9.9	−8.2	−2.6	−0.3	−3.3	−0	0.2	−3.8	3.5
1958	−8.0	−8.0	−6.3	−0.8	1.5	−1.3	2.0	2.4	−1.5	5.8
1959	−5.9	−5.8	−4.1	1.5	3.8	1.1	4.5	4.9	1.3	8.5
1960	−6.3	−6.2	−4.5	0.8	3.0	0.4	3.6	3.9	0.4	7.2
1961	−4.9	−4.8	−3.1	2.1	4.3	1.8	5.0	5.4	2.1	8.8
1962	−4.6	−4.5	−2.8	2.3	4.4	2.0	5.1	5.5	2.2	8.7
1963	−4.5	−4.4	−2.7	2.2	4.3	1.9	4.9	5.3	2.2	8.3
1964	−4.5	−4.4	−2.8	1.9	3.9	1.7	4.5	4.8	1.8	7.7
1965	−3.6	−3.4	−1.8	2.9	4.9	2.7	5.5	5.9	3.0	8.8
1966	−2.2	−2.0	−0.4	4.2	6.2	4.1	6.9	7.3	4.5	10.3
1967	−1.0	−0.8	0.8	5.4	7.4	5.4	8.2	8.6	6.0	11.6
1968	−2.2	−2.0	−0.5	3.9	5.8	3.8	6.4	6.8	4.1	9.5
1969	−2.1	−2.0	−0.5	3.8	5.6	3.7	6.2	6.6	4.0	9.2
1970	−2.1	−1.9	−0.5	3.7	5.4	3.6	6.0	6.4	3.9	8.9
1971	−3.3	−3.2	−1.7	2.2	3.8	2.0	4.3	4.6	2.2	6.8
1972	−3.5	−3.3	−2.0	1.9	3.4	1.6	3.9	4.1	1.8	6.3
1973	−5.6	−5.5	−4.3	−0.6	0.8	−1.0	1.0	1.2	−1.1	3.1
1974	−6.9	−6.8	−5.7	−2.2	−0.9	−2.6	−0.7	−0.6	−2.9	1.1
1975	−8.9	−8.9	−7.9	−4.6	−3.4	−5.1	−3.3	−3.3	−5.5	−1.8
1976	−10.5	−10.5	−9.5	−6.4	−5.3	−7.0	−5.3	−5.3	−7.5	−4.0
1977	−8.2	−8.2	−7.2	−4.0	−2.8	−4.5	−2.8	−2.7	−4.8	−1.3
1978	−11.3	−11.3	−10.5	−7.5	−6.5	−8.1	−6.6	−6.6	−8.7	−5.5

Table B.2 (continued)

End year	Beginning year									
	1939	1940	1941	1942	1943	1944	1945	1946	1947	1948
1939	−23.1									
1940	−32.1	−40.0								
1941	−41.0	−48.4	−55.6							
1942	−43.4	−48.9	−52.9	−50.0						
1943	−27.2	−28.1	−23.7	0	100.0					
1944	−23.2	−23.2	−18.4	0	41.4	0				
1945	5.3	11.0	25.5	62.7	141.0	164.6	600.0			
1946	9.4	15.0	28.2	58.5	111.5	115.4	216.2	42.9		
1947	−0.9	2.3	10.4	28.5	55.2	45.6	65.1	−19.8	−55.0	
1948	−4.0	−1.6	4.7	18.3	36.6	26.6	34.3	−22.6	−43.0	−27.8
1949	−11.6	−10.4	−6.3	2.8	14.0	3.8	4.6	−35.0	−50.0	−47.3
1950	−5.4	−3.6	1.2	10.7	22.3	14.0	16.5	−18.6	−29.3	−17.8
1951	−3.1	−1.2	3.4	12.5	23.1	15.9	18.3	−12.0	−20.1	−7.8
1952	−7.5	−6.2	−2.7	4.5	12.5	5.5	6.3	−18.8	−26.1	−18.4
1953	−4.4	−2.9	0.8	7.9	15.8	9.6	10.7	−12.1	−18.0	−9.3
1954	0.7	2.6	6.6	14.0	22.1	16.8	18.6	−2.6	−7.2	2.9
1955	2.6	4.4	8.4	15.5	23.2	18.3	20.1	0.7	−3.1	6.6
1956	1.4	3.1	6.6	13.0	19.8	15.1	16.5	−1.0	−4.6	3.7
1957	3.9	5.6	9.2	15.5	22.1	17.9	19.4	3.0	−0	8.3
1958	6.2	8.0	11.6	17.8	24.3	20.4	22.0	6.7	4.1	12.4
1959	9.0	11.0	14.6	20.9	27.2	23.7	25.5	11.0	8.8	17.1
1960	7.7	9.5	12.8	18.5	24.3	20.8	22.3	8.9	6.8	14.1
1961	9.3	11.0	14.3	19.9	25.5	22.3	23.8	11.1	9.2	16.1
1962	9.2	10.8	14.0	19.2	24.5	21.4	22.7	10.8	9.1	15.7
1963	8.8	10.4	13.3	18.3	23.2	20.3	21.4	10.2	8.5	14.6
1964	8.2	9.6	12.4	17.1	21.7	18.8	19.9	9.2	7.6	13.3
1965	9.2	10.7	13.4	17.9	22.4	19.7	20.8	10.6	9.1	14.6
1966	10.7	12.3	15.0	19.4	23.9	21.3	22.4	12.6	11.3	16.7
1967	12.1	13.7	16.4	20.8	25.1	22.7	23.8	14.4	13.2	18.6
1968	9.9	11.2	13.7	17.8	21.7	19.3	20.2	11.3	10.1	14.9
1969	9.6	10.9	13.2	17.1	20.8	18.5	19.3	10.8	9.6	14.1
1970	9.2	10.5	12.8	16.4	20.0	17.8	18.5	10.4	9.2	13.5
1971	7.1	8.3	10.3	13.7	17.0	14.8	15.4	7.6	6.4	10.3
1972	6.6	7.6	9.6	12.9	16.0	13.8	14.3	6.9	5.7	9.4
1973	3.3	4.2	5.9	8.8	11.6	9.4	9.8	2.8	1.5	4.7
1974	1.2	2.0	3.6	6.3	8.8	6.7	6.9	0.2	1.0	1.9
1975	−1.8	−1.1	0.3	2.7	5.0	2.9	3.0	−3.4	4.7	−2.1
1976	−4.1	−3.5	−2.2	−0	2.1	−0	−0	−6.1	−7.4	−5.1
1977	−1.2	−0.6	0.8	3.1	5.3	3.3	3.4	−2.6	−3.8	−1.3
1978	−5.5	−5.0	−3.9	−1.9	−0	−2.0	−2.0	−7.7	−8.9	−6.8

Table B.4 Percentage of Chicago Board of Trade seat price changes for all yearly holding periods from 1929 to 1978

End year	Beginning year									
	1929	1930	1931	1932	1933	1934	1935	1936	1937	1938
1929	−37.7									
1930	−50.4	−60.5								
1931	−36.0	−35.1	6.7							
1932	−41.4	−42.6	−30.7	−55.0						
1933	−26.0	−22.8	−3.5	−8.2	87.5					
1934	−23.7	−20.6	−5.4	−9.1	29.1	−11.1				
1935	−21.2	−18.1	−5.2	−7.9	16.9	−7.7	−4.2			
1936	−20.2	−17.4	−6.5	−9.0	8.6	−9.5	−8.7	−13.0		
1937	−23.0	−20.9	−12.7	−15.6	−4.2	−19.0	−21.5	−29.0	−42.0	
1938	−26.0	−24.6	−18.2	−21.3	−13.6	−26.0	−29.3	−36.1	−45.2	−48.3
1939	−21.6	−19.8	−13.2	−15.4	−7.4	−17.7	−18.9	−22.3	−25.1	−14.9
1940	−29.6	−28.8	−24.5	−27.4	−22.9	−32.1	−35.1	−39.9	−45.2	−46.3
1941	−32.1	−31.6	−28.1	−30.9	−27.5	−35.6	−38.5	−42.9	−47.5	−48.8
1942	−31.6	−31.1	−27.8	−30.3	−27.2	−34.5	−36.9	−40.6	−44.3	−44.7
1943	−20.4	−19.0	−14.4	−15.9	−11.0	−17.4	−18.1	−19.6	−20.5	−16.3
1944	−13.3	−11.4	−6.1	−7.0	−1.2	−6.8	−6.4	−6.6	−5.8	1.0
1945	−11.8	−9.9	−4.8	−5.5	−0	−5.1	−4.5	−4.6	−3.6	2.7
1946	−11.0	−9.1	−4.2	−4.9	0.3	−4.4	−3.8	−3.8	−2.8	2.9
1947	−10.8	−9.0	−4.4	−5.0	−0.2	−4.6	−4.1	−4.1	−3.2	1.9
1948	−10.3	−8.5	−4.1	−4.7	−0.2	−4.3	−3.8	−3.7	−2.9	1.7
1949	−11.8	−10.2	−6.3	−6.9	−2.9	−6.8	−6.5	−6.6	−6.1	−2.3
1950	−11.3	−9.7	−5.9	−6.6	−2.7	−6.4	−6.1	−6.2	−5.7	−2.1
1951	−10.3	−8.8	−5.1	−5.7	−1.9	−5.4	−5.0	−5.1	−4.5	−1.1
1952	−9.5	−8.0	−4.4	−4.9	−1.2	−4.5	−4.1	−4.1	−3.6	−0.2
1953	−7.4	−5.8	−2.2	−2.6	1.1	−2.0	−1.5	−1.4	−0.6	2.8
1954	−6.1	−4.5	−0.9	−1.2	2.3	−0.6	−0	0.2	1.0	4.4
1955	−5.9	−4.4	−1.0	−1.3	2.2	−0.6	−0.1	0.1	0.9	4.0
1956	−5.0	−3.5	−0.1	−0.4	3.0	0.3	0.9	1.1	1.9	4.9
1957	−6.2	−4.8	−0.2	−1.9	1.2	−1.4	−1.0	−0.8	−0.2	2.6
1958	−6.5	−5.2	−0.2	−2.5	0.4	−2.1	−1.7	−1.6	−1.0	1.5
1959	−4.7	−3.4	−0.3	−0.6	2.4	0	0.5	0.7	1.3	3.9
1960	−6.2	−4.9	−2.1	−2.4	0.4	−1.9	−1.5	−1.4	−0.9	1.4
1961	−4.4	−3.2	−0.3	−0.5	2.2	0	0.5	0.6	1.2	3.6
1962	−3.6	−2.3	0.5	0.3	3.0	0.9	1.4	1.6	2.2	4.6
1963	−2.2	−0.9	1.9	1.7	4.5	2.5	3.0	3.2	3.9	6.2
1964	−2.2	−0.9	1.8	1.7	4.3	2.4	2.9	3.1	3.7	6.0
1965	−2.5	−1.3	1.4	1.2	3.7	1.8	2.3	2.5	3.1	5.2
1966	−1.1	0.1	2.7	2.6	5.1	3.3	3.8	4.1	4.7	6.8
1967	−1.1	0	2.6	2.5	4.9	3.2	3.6	3.9	4.5	6.6
1968	−2.1	−0.9	1.5	1.4	3.7	1.9	2.4	2.6	3.1	5.0
1969	0.8	2.0	4.5	4.5	6.9	5.2	5.7	6.0	6.7	8.7
1970	0.3	1.4	3.9	3.8	6.1	4.5	4.9	5.2	5.8	7.7
1971	−0	1.1	3.4	3.4	5.6	4.0	4.4	4.7	5.3	7.1
1972	0.3	1.4	3.7	3.7	5.9	4.3	4.8	5.0	5.6	7.4
1973	1.2	2.3	4.6	4.6	6.7	5.2	5.7	6.0	6.5	8.3
1974	2.0	3.1	5.4	5.4	7.5	6.1	6.5	6.8	7.4	9.2
1975	3.0	4.2	6.5	6.4	8.6	7.2	7.7	8.0	8.6	10.4
1976	2.9	4.0	6.2	6.2	8.3	6.9	7.4	7.7	8.3	10.1
1977	3.3	4.4	0.6	6.6	8.6	7.3	7.8	8.1	8.6	10.4
1978	3.9	5.0	0.2	7.2	9.2	7.9	8.4	8.7	9.3	11.0

Table B.4 (continued)

End year	Beginning year									
	1939	1940	1941	1942	1943	1944	1945	1946	1947	1948
1939	40.0									
1940	−45.2	−78.6								
1941	−48.9	−69.1	−55.6							
1942	−43.8	−58.5	−42.3	−25.0						
1943	−7.8	−16.9	30.5	123.6	566.7					
1944	12.9	8.1	62.0	149.3	354.6	210.0				
1945	13.3	9.4	51.6	106.0	188.5	89.7	16.1			
1946	12.1	8.6	42.4	79.7	123.6	55.4	10.0	4.2		
1947	9.9	6.6	34.0	61.1	87.8	36.8	4.1	−4.1	−6.7	
1948	8.8	5.8	29.2	50.5	69.0	28.5	3.1	−0.9	−3.4	−0
1949	3.5	0.5	19.3	34.9	46.8	14.0	−6.6	−11.6	−16.3	−20.7
1950	3.2	0.4	17.2	30.5	39.9	11.9	−5.5	−9.4	−12.5	−14.3
1951	4.0	1.5	16.9	28.7	36.7	12.1	−3.0	−5.9	−7.8	−8.1
1952	4.6	2.2	16.5	27.1	34.0	12.1	−1.3	−3.5	−4.8	−4.4
1953	7.6	5.6	19.4	29.6	36.2	16.2	4.2	2.8	2.6	4.3
1954	9.1	7.2	20.3	29.9	36.0	17.7	6.8	5.8	6.1	8.0
1955	8.4	6.7	18.7	27.3	32.6	15.9	6.0	5.1	5.2	6.7
1956	9.1	7.6	19.0	27.0	31.9	16.5	7.3	6.6	6.8	8.4
1957	6.3	4.7	14.9	22.0	26.0	11.9	3.4	2.4	2.3	3.2
1958	5.0	3.4	12.9	19.3	22.8	9.7	1.8	0.8	0.5	1.2
1959	7.5	6.1	15.4	21.6	25.2	12.7	5.4	4.6	4.7	5.7
1960	4.6	3.1	11.5	17.1	20.0	8.5	1.6	0.7	0.5	1.0
1961	6.8	5.5	13.8	19.3	22.2	11.2	4.7	4.1	4.0	4.9
1962	7.7	6.5	14.5	19.8	22.6	12.2	6.0	5.4	5.5	6.4
1963	9.3	8.2	16.1	21.3	24.1	14.1	8.3	7.8	8.1	9.1
1964	9.0	7.9	15.4	20.3	22.9	13.4	7.8	7.4	7.6	8.5
1965	8.0	6.9	14.0	18.6	21.0	12.0	6.7	6.2	6.3	7.1
1966	9.6	8.7	15.7	20.2	22.5	13.8	8.8	8.4	8.7	9.5
1967	9.2	8.3	15.0	19.3	21.5	13.2	8.3	8.0	8.2	9.0
1968	7.5	6.6	12.8	16.8	18.8	10.9	6.2	5.9	5.9	6.5
1969	11.3	10.5	16.9	21.0	23.2	15.5	11.0	10.8	11.1	12.0
1970	10.2	9.4	15.5	19.4	21.4	14.0	9.6	9.4	9.6	10.4
1971	9.5	8.7	14.5	18.2	20.0	12.9	8.8	8.5	8.7	9.4
1972	9.7	8.9	14.6	18.1	19.9	13.0	9.0	8.8	9.0	9.6
1973	10.7	9.9	15.5	19.0	20.8	14.1	10.2	10.0	10.2	10.9
1974	11.5	10.8	16.3	19.7	21.5	15.0	11.2	11.1	11.3	12.0
1975	12.7	12.0	17.4	20.8	22.6	16.3	12.7	12.6	12.9	13.6
1976	12.2	11.6	16.8	20.1	21.7	15.6	12.1	12.0	12.2	13.0
1977	12.5	11.9	17.0	20.2	21.8	15.9	12.5	12.4	12.6	13.3
1978	13.1	12.5	7.6	20.7	22.3	16.5	13.2	13.1	13.4	14.1

Table B.4 (continued)

End year	Beginning year									
	1949	1950	1951	1952	1953	1954	1955	1956	1957	1958
1949	−37.1									
1950	−20.7	−0								
1951	−10.6	6.6	13.6							
1952	−5.4	8.4	12.8	12.0						
1953	5.2	19.6	26.9	34.2	60.7					
1954	9.4	22.2	28.5	33.9	46.4	33.3				
1955	7.7	17.9	21.8	23.9	28.2	14.5	−1.7			
1956	9.5	18.6	22.0	23.7	26.9	17.2	9.9	22.9		
1957	3.6	10.2	11.8	11.5	11.4	1.6	−7.2	−9.8	−33.8	
1958	1.3	6.9	7.8	6.9	6.1	−2.3	−9.6	−12.2	−25.7	−16.7
1959	6.2	11.9	13.4	13.3	13.5	7.1	2.5	3.6	−2.1	19.0
1960	1.1	5.6	6.2	5.4	4.6	−1.7	−6.5	−7.5	−13.8	−5.9
1961	5.2	9.9	10.8	10.5	10.4	5.3	1.8	2.4	−1.3	9.1
1962	6.9	11.3	12.3	12.2	12.2	7.8	5.0	6.0	3.4	13.0
1963	9.7	14.1	15.3	15.4	15.8	12.0	9.9	11.4	9.9	19.5
1964	9.0	13.1	14.1	14.2	14.3	10.8	8.8	10.0	8.5	16.5
1965	7.5	11.2	12.0	11.9	11.8	8.5	6.5	7.4	5.8	12.1
1966	10.1	13.8	14.7	14.8	15.0	12.1	10.4	11.6	10.5	17.0
1967	9.5	12.9	13.7	13.7	13.8	11.0	9.5	10.5	9.4	15.0
1968	6.9	9.9	10.5	10.3	10.2	7.5	5.8	6.4	5.2	9.7
1969	12.6	15.9	16.8	17.0	17.3	15.0	13.9	15.0	14.5	19.8
1970	10.9	13.9	14.7	14.7	14.9	12.6	11.5	12.4	11.7	16.3
1971	9.8	12.6	13.2	13.2	13.3	11.1	9.9	10.7	9.9	14.0
1972	10.1	12.8	13.4	13.4	13.5	11.4	10.3	11.0	10.3	14.2
1973	11.4	14.1	14.7	14.8	14.9	13.0	12.0	12.9	12.3	16.1
1974	12.5	15.2	15.9	16.0	16.1	14.4	13.5	14.4	13.9	17.6
1975	14.2	16.8	17.5	17.7	18.0	16.3	15.6	16.5	16.2	19.9
1976	13.5	16.0	16.6	16.7	17.0	15.3	14.6	15.4	15.1	18.5
1977	13.8	16.3	16.9	17.1	17.3	15.7	15.0	15.8	15.5	18.8
1978	14.6	17.0	17.7	17.8	18.1	16.6	16.0	16.8	16.5	19.7

Table B.4 (continued)

End year	Beginning year									
	1959	1960	1961	1962	1963	1964	1965	1966	1967	1968
1959	70.0									
1960	−0	−41.2								
1961	19.3	0	70.0							
1962	22.0	9.2	48.7	30.1						
1963	28.5	19.8	51.8	43.5	58.2					
1964	.23.1	15.5	36.7	27.1	25.5	−0.4				
1965	17.0	9.9	24.6	15.3	10.7	−7.4	−14.0			
1966	22.1	16.5	30.5	23.8	22.2	12.2	19.0	64.6		
1967	19.2	14.1	25.4	19.2	17.1	8.6	11.8	27.5	−1.3	
1968	12.7	7.7	16.2	10.0	7.0	−1.1	−1.3	3.4	−18.1	−32.1
1969	23.8	20.0	29.9	25.6	24.9	20.1	24.7	36.8	28.6	46.8
1970	19.5	15.8	23.9	19.6	18.3	13.5	16.0	23.2	14.5	20.4
1971	16.8	13.2	20.1	16.0	14.5	10.0	11.6	16.5	8.7	11.4
1972	16.8	13.4	19.8	16.1	14.7	10.7	12.2	16.5	10.0	12.4
1973	18.6	15.6	21.8	18.5	17.5	14.0	15.7	20.1	14.8	17.8
1974	20.2	17.4	23.3	20.3	19.6	16.6	18.4	22.7	18.2	21.3
1975	22.4	20.0	25.8	23.1	22.6	20.0	22.1	26.4	22.8	26.1
1976	20.8	18.4	23.7	21.1	20.5	18.0	19.6	23.3	19.8	22.4
1977	21.0	18.8	23.8	21.3	20.8	18.5	20.0	23.4	20.2	22.6
1978	21.9	19.8	24.6	22.4	21.9	19.8	21.4	24.6	21.8	24.1

End year	Beginning year									
	1969	1970	1971	1972	1973	1974	1975	1976	1977	1978
1969	217.0									
1970	60.2	−19.0								
1971	31.3	−15.5	−11.8							
1972	27.5	−5.9	1.5	16.7						
1973	31.4	5.5	15.2	31.2	48.6					
1974	33.6	12.4	22.1	36.0	46.9	45.2				
1975	37.8	19.9	29.7	42.9	52.9	55.0	65.6			
1976	31.7	16.2	23.4	32.0	36.1	32.1	26.1	−4.0		
1977	30.9	17.2	23.6	30.8	33.8	30.3	25.7	9.5	25.0	
1978	31.8	19.6	25.6	32.0	34.8	32.2	29.1	18.9	32.3	40.0

Appendix C:
Comparison of NYSE and Phlx Seat Prices

Table C.1 Ratio of the NYSE seat prices to the Phlx seat prices from 1929 to 1978

	Number	Phlx	NYSE	Ratio
6–1929	1	$39,000.000	$394,999.995	10.128
12–1929	2	36,500.000	419,999.993	11.507
	3	36,500.000	467,999.994	12.822
	4	20,000.000	199,999.997	10.000
	5	6,000.000	224,999.996	37.500
	6	4,000.000	131,999.998	33.000
	7	2,000.000	79,999.999	40.000
	8	2,200.000	102,999.998	46.818
	9	5,100.000	229,999.997	45.098
	10	4,500.000	124,999.998	27.778
	11	3,500.000	95,999.999	27.429
12–1934	12	2,000.000	94,999.999	47.500
	13	1,200.000	107,999.998	90.000
	14	1,900.000	144,999.998	76.316
	15	4,500.000	124,999.998	27.778
	16	4,500.000	⬥ 128,999.998	28.667
	17	2,750.000	88,999.999	32.364
	18	1,000.000	74,999.999	75.000
	19	800.000	64,999.999	81.250
	20	975.000	69,999.999	71.795
	21	1,000.000	61,999.999	62.000
12–1939	22	750.000	61,999.999	82.667
	23	700.000	40,000.000	57.143
	24	450.000	32,000.000	0.001
	25	200.000	28,000.000	140.000
	26	200.000	25,000.000	125.000
	27	100.000	18,000.000	180.000
	28	100.000	28,000.000	280.000
	29	200.000	40,000.000	200.000
	30	200.000	47,000.000	235.000
	31	200.000	59,999.999	300.000
12–1944	32	200.000	64,999.999	325.000
	33	200.000	74,999.999	375.000
	34	1,400.000	94,999.999	67.857
	35	2,750.000	83,999.999	30.545
	36	2,000.000	69,999.999	35.000
	37	2,000.000	61,999.999	31.000
	38	900.000	60,999.999	67.778
	39	900.000	67,999.999	75.556
	40	650.000	42,000.000	64.615
	41	300.000	35,000.000	116.667

Table C.1 (continued)

	Number	Phlx	NYSE	Ratio
12–1949	42	$ 250.000	$ 47,999.999	192.000
	43	300.000	52,999.999	176.667
	44	500.000	51,999.999	104.000
	45	625.000	55,999.999	89.600
	46	650.000	53,999.999	83.077
	47	400.000	43,999.999	110.000
	48	325.000	50,999.999	156.923
	49	500.000	48,999.999	98.000
	50	500.000	45,999.999	92.000
	51	300.000	50,999.999	170.000
12–1954	52	1,100.000	89,999.999	81.818
	53	2,000.000	89,999.999	45.000
	54	1,500.000	88,999.999	59.333
	55	1,200.000	104,999.998	87.500
	56	1,250.000	84,999.999	68.000
	57	2,000.000	79,999.999	40.000
	58	2,000.000	69,999.999	35.000
	59	2,000.000	89,999.999	45.000
	60	3,250.000	138,999.998	42.769
	61	6,500.000	152,999.998	23.538
12–1959	62	6,000.000	159,999.998	26.667
	63	6,000.000	144,999.998	24.167
	64	5,000.000	149,999.998	30.000
	65	8,500.000	194,999.997	22.941
	66	7,500.000	209,999.997	28.000
	67	10,000.000	139,999.998	14.000
	68	8,000.000	184,999.997	23.125
	69	8,500.000	204,999.997	24.118
	70	8,000.000	204,999.997	25.625
	71	6,500.000	206,999.996	31.846
12–1964	72	7,500.000	204,999.997	27.333
	73	7,000.000	194,999.997	27.857
	74	10,500.000	229,999.997	21.905
	75	15,000.000	249,999.996	16.667
	76	17,000.000	219,999.996	12.941
	77	16,500.000	354,999.995	21.515
	78	27,000.000	449,999.993	16.667
	79	30,000.000	434,999.993	14.500
	80	16,500.000	514,999.993	31.212
	81	16,500.000	499,999.993	30.303

Table C.1 (continued)

	Number	Phlx	NYSE	Ratio
12–1969	82	16,500.000	319,999.997	19.394
	83	16,500.000	174,999.997	10.606
	84	16,500.000	174,999.997	10.606
	85	11,000.000	199,999.997	18.182
	86	9,500.000	199,999.997	21.053
	87	8,000.000	204,999.997	25.625
	88	8,500.000	179,999.998	21.176
	89	3,500.000	71,999.999	20.571
	90	3,000.000	109,999.998	36.667
	91	2,600.000	71,999.999	27.692
12–1974	92	1,500.000	74,999.999	50.000
	93	2,000.000	129,999.998	65.000
	94	500.000	54,999.999	110.000
	95	500.000	84,999.999	170.000
	96	200.000	79,999.999	400.000
	97	100.000	51,999.999	520.000
	98	600.000	44,999.999	75.000
	99	100.000	57,999.999	580.000
12–1978	100	100.000	74,999.999	750.000

Notes

Chapter 2

1. See, for example, Gabriel Kolko, *Railroads and Regulation, 1877–1916* (Princeton, N.J., 1965) and Gabriel Kolko, *The Triumph of Conservatism: A Reinterpretation of American History, 1900–1916* (New York, 1963).

2. Thomas McCraw, "Regulation in America: A Review Article," *Business History Review,* vol. 49 (summer 1975), pp. 159–183.

3. For discussion and further reference to the market failure view of regulation, see C. F. Phillips, *The Economics of Regulation* (Homewood, Ill.: Irwin, 1969). This view draws heavily on the early work of A. C. Pigov, *The Economics of Welfare,* 4th ed. (London: Macmillan, 1932).

4. See, for example, Murray Weidenbaum, "Four Questions for OSHA," *Labor Law Journal,* vol. 30, no. 8, 1979.

5. For a review of recent developments in assessing the effectiveness of regulatory programs, see American Enterprise Institute, *Proposals for Ranking the Effectiveness of Government Programs* (Washington, D.C., 1980).

6. U.S., Congress, Senate Committe on Banking and Currency, *Stock Exchange Practices: Hearings before the Committee on Banking and Currency,* April 11, 1932–May 3, 1934, pursuant to Senate resolutions 84, 56, and 97, 72nd Congress, 73rd Congress. U.S., Congress, Senate Committee on Banking and Currency, *Stock Exchange Practices: Report of Committee on Banking and Currency,* 73rd Congress, 2nd session, 1934, S. Rept. 1455.

7. See George J. Benston, "Required Disclosure and the Stock Market: An Evaluation of the Securities Exchange Act of 1934," *American Economics Review,* vol. 63 (March 1973).

8. Roger Noll, *Reforming Regulation* (The Brookings Institution, Washington, D.C., 1971), p. viii.

9. President's Advisory Council on Executive Organizations, *A New Regulatory Framework: Report on Selected Independent Regulatory Agencies* (Washington, D.C.: Government Printing Office, 1971).

10. Richard Schmalensee, *The Control of Natural Monopolies* (Lexington, Mass.: Lexington Books, 1979).

11. Homer Kripke, *The SEC and Corporate Disclosure: Regulation in Search of a Purpose* (New York: Harcourt Brace Jovanovich, 1979).

12. The evolution of this theory is revealed in George Stigler, "The Theory of Economic Regulation," *Bell Journal of Economics and Management Science,* vol. 2 (spring, 1971); R. A. Posner, "Taxation by Regulation," *Bell Journal of Economics and Management Science,* vol. 2 (spring 1971); Sam Peltzman, "Toward a More General Theory of Regulation," *Journal of Law and Economics,* vol. 19 (August 1976); and Robert E. McCormick and Robert D. Tollison, *Politicians, Legislators, and the Economist: An Inquiry into the Interest Group Theory of Government* (unpublished manuscript).

Chapter 3

1. The corporate disclosure system is only one of three major reporting systems administered by the SEC, the other two being reports from investment managers and advisors and reports from brokers and dealers.

2. One argument for mandating corporate disclosure is that in a free market too little information would be produced, due to the externalities of information. While one group pays, the nonpaying groups also benefit.

3. For a review of this literature, see E. Fama, "Efficient Capital Markets: A Review of Theory and Empirical Work," *Journal of Finance,* vol. 25 (May 1970), pp. 338–417; and Richard Roll, "A Critique of the Cost Pricing Theory's Test, Part 1: On Past and Potential Testability of the Theory," *Journal of Financial Economics,* vol. 4 (March 1977)), pp. 129–176.

4. U.S., Congress, Senate Committee on Banking and Currency. *Stock Exchange Practices: Letter from the Counsel of the Committee on Banking and Currency,* 73rd Congress, 1st session, February 18, 1933.

5. *Yale Review,* 1933, pp. 532–534.

6. Report of the Advisory Committee on Corporate Disclosure to the Securities and Exchange Commission (Washington, D.C.: Government Printing Office, 1978).

7. However, it is possible that a more accurately priced security would have a larger residual variance in the case where the additional information causes larger or more frequent reassessment of the stock's value.

8. George J. Benston, "Required Disclosure and the Stock Market: An Evaluation of the Securities Exchange Act of 1934," *American Economic Review,* vol. 63 (March 1973).

9. Ibid., p. 149.

10. Ibid., p. 151.

11. Ibid., p. 152.

12. Ibid., p.. 153.

13. Ibid., p. 136.

14. George Stigler, "Public Regulation of the Securities Markets," *Journal of Business* (April 1964), p. 124.

15. Irwin Friend and Edward S. Herman, "Through a Looking Glass Darkly," *Journal of Business,* vol. 37 (October 1964).

16. For example see: Sidney Robbins and Walter Werner, "Professor Stigler Revisited," *Journal of Business,* vol. 37 (October 1964), pp. 406–413; George J. Stigler, "The SEC Through a Glass Darkly: Comments," *Journal of Business,* vol. 37 (October 1964), pp. 414–422; and Irwin Friend and Edward S. Herman, "Professor Stigler on Securities Regulation: A Further Comment," *Journal of Business,* vol. 38 (January 1965), pp. 106–110.

17. Stigler, "The SEC," p. 419.

18. L. Fisher and J. H. Lorie, "Some Studies of the Variability of Returns on Investments in Common Stock," *Journal of Business* (April 1970), pp. 99–134.

19. George J. Benston, "The Value of the SEC's Accounting Disclosure Requirements," *The Accounting Review* (July 1969), pp. 515–532. (Also reported in George J. Benston, "The Effectiveness and Effects of the SEC's Accounting Disclosure Requirements," in Henry G. Manne, ed., *Economic Policy and the Regulation of Corporate Securities* (Washington, D.C.: American Enterprise Institute, 1969), pp. 23–79.

20. Ibid., pp. 525–526.

21. Ibid., pp. 526–528.

22. For a detailed discussion of insider trading, see Henry Manne, *Insider Trading and the Stock Market* (Riverside, N.Y.: Free Press, 1966); and Henry Manne (ed.), *Economic Policy and the Regulation of Corporate Securities* (Washington, D.C.: American Enterprise Institute, 1969).

23. U.S. Congress, House Committee on Interstate and Foreign Commerce, *Report of the Advisory Committee on Corporate Disclosure to the Securities and Exchange Commission,* 95th Congress, 1st session, Committee Print 95-29 (Washington, D.C.: Government Printing Office, November 3, 1977), p. 290.

24. Ibid., p. 291.

25. Calculated from Attachment 1-A, ibid., p. 30.

26. Ibid., p. 252.

27. Calculated from ibid., p. 62.

28. For example, see tables G-VV, ibid., pp. 100–144.

29. Benston, *Corporate Financial Disclosure in the U.S. and U.K.,* p. 152.

30. See, for example, O. E. Williamson, *The Economics of Discretionary Behavior: Management Objectives in a Theory of the Firm* (Englewood Cliffs, N.J.: Prentice-Hall, Inc., 1964), and B. Hinberg, "Separation of Ownership and Control in the Modern Corporation," *The Journal of Law and Economics* (April 1972), pp. 185–222.

31. M. C. Jensen and W. H. Meckling, "Theory of the Firm: Managerial Behavior, Agency Costs, and Ownership Structure," *Journal of Financial Economics* (October 1976), pp. 305–360.

32. The full set of assumptions underlying figure 3.1 are:
   (a) Permanent assumptions
      • All taxes are zero.
      • No trade credit is available.
      • All outside equity shares are nonvoting.
      • No complex financial claims such as convertible bonds or preferred stock or warrants can be issued.
      • No outside owner gains utility from ownership in a firm in any way other than through its effect on the owner's wealth or cash flows.
      • All dynamic aspects of the multiperiod nature of the problem are ignored by assuming there is only one production-financing decision to be made by the entrepreneur.
      • The entrepreneur-manager's money wages are held constant throughout the analysis.
      • There exists a single manager (the peak coordinator) with ownership interest in the firm.

(b) Temporary assumptions
- The size of the firm is fixed.
- No monitoring or bonding activities are possible.
- No debt financing through bonds, preferred stock, or personal borrowing (secured or unsecured) is possible.
- All elements of the owner-manager's decision problem involving portfolio considerations induced by the presence of uncertainty and the existence of diversifiable risk are ignored.

33. The discussion in this section draws heavily from Jensen and Meckling, "Theory of the Firm," pp. 305–360.

34. Jensen and Meckling, p. 312.

35. See Jensen and Meckling, p. 318.

36. An expanded and continuing effort to measure these costs at the SEC would contribute greatly to a better estimation and understanding of these costs. There appears to be some interest in further cost studies at the SEC.

Chapter 4

The authors gratefully acknowledge the extensive assistance of Kim Korn and Dan Roberts in preparing this chapter as well as the constructive and thoughtful suggestions of Lawrence J. White, Michael Mann, Robert W. Swinarton, Joshua Ronen, and other participants in the NYU Deregulation Conference for an earlier paper on the same subject (Dan Roberts, Susan M. Phillips, and J. Richard Zecher, "Deregulation of the NYSE Fixed Commission Rate Structure," *The Deregulation of the Banking and Securities Industries,* Lexington, Mass.: Lexington Books, 1979).

1. U.S., Securities and Exchange Commission, *Report of the Special Study of the Securities Markets* (July 17, 1963), pp. 347, 350.

2. SEC release no. 8239 (1968), p. 4.

3. SEC release no. 8239 (1968), p. 4.

4. For a summary of the NYSE position on give-ups, see the letter to the commission from Robert W. Haack, president of the New York Stock Exchange, January 2, 1968, reprinted in SEC release no. 8239 (1968).

5. SEC release no. 8239 (1968).

6. SEC release no. 8324 (1968).

7. NYSE, "Economic Effects of Negotiated Commissions on the Brokerage Industry, the Market for Corporate Securities, and the Investing Public" (August 1968).

8. Michael Mann, "A Critique of the New York Stock Exchange's Report on the Economic Effects of Negotiated Commission Rates on the Brokerage Industry, the Market for Corporate Securities and the Investing Public," prepared for the Justice Department (October 1968), p. 57.

9. *Silver v. New York Stock Exchange*, 393 U.S. 341 (1963). Surprisingly the SEC testified on behalf of the NYSE, defending the exchange's immunity from the Sherman Antitrust Act. The NYSE lost the case, however.

10. U.S., Department of Justice, "Memorandum of the United States Department of Justice on the Fixed Minimum Commission State Structure," statement submitted to the SEC (January 17, 1969), pp. 9–14.

11. NYSE, "The Economics of Minimum Commission Rates" (May 1, 1969).

12. U.S., Securities and Exchange Commission, *Institutional Investor Study Report,* summary volume (1971), pp. 104–105.

13. U.S., Congress, Senate Subcommittee on Securities, *Securities Industry Study.* Final report of the Subcommittee on Securities to the Committee on Banking, Housing, and Urban Affairs, 93d Congress, 1st session (February 1973), p. 44; and U.S., Congress, House Subcommittee on Commerce and Finance of the Committee on Interstate and Foreign Commerce, 93d Congress, 1st session (February 1973), pp. 131–132.

14. SEC release no. 8860 (1970).

15. SEC release no. 9007 (1970).

16. U.S., Congress, House *Securities Industry Study* (1973), pp. 136–143; and U.S., Congress, Senate final *Securities Industry Study* (1973), pp. 44–61.

17. The SEC said that it did not approve the 1971 rate increase but that at most would give an interlocutory nonobjection (Senate interim *Securities Industry Study,* 1973, p. 58).

18. Sam Peltzman, "Toward a More General Theory of Regulation," *Journal of Law and Economics,* vol. 19 (August 1976), pp. 211–240.

19. These variables are consistent with those used by Peltzman.

20. See appendix A for the documentation of the interpolation methods.

21. See table A.9 (appendix A) for a documentation of the proportions of public volume executed by individuals and institutions.

22. This assumption may be somewhat conservative.

23. The variation of the distribution of the volume over the various trade sizes is documented in tables A.7 through A.9, appendix A.

24. The cost of execution is documented for the actual share price in table A.10, appendix A, and for the $20/$35 assumption in table A.11.

25. The SEC has recently released the commission date for 1978, and a production function for 1978, comparable to the one for 1977 used in this analysis, shifted only slightly downward. The shift was more pronounced for institutions than individuals. The shape of the curve, however, did not change.

26. To the extent that give-ups are directed to affiliates of investors, they more closely approximate rebates and thus a form of price competition.

27. As indicated in table 4.5, the proportion of the commission that had to be bartered away through nonprice competition got as high as 70 percent for institutions.

28. Peltzman, "Toward a More General," p. 227.

29. Peltzman, "Toward a More General," p. 227.

30. Peltzman, "Toward a More General," pp. 235–236.

31. This may be due to the importance of the more lightly taxed individual business engaged in by publicly owned firms. In fact fixed rates may have discriminated against retail firms to the advantage of institutional firms.

32. An examination of the beta values and variance of returns of six publicly traded brokerage firms 33 months before and 32 months after deregulation produced the following observations: (1) four had beta increases and two had beta decreases, (2) four variance decreases and two variance increases, and (3) three average return increases and three average return decreases. Four of the six firms had conflicting risk signals

(beta and variance), indicating increased as well as decreased risk; but none of the results were significant. We cannot therefore conclude that there was a consistent pattern of risk or return for these brokerage firms before and after deregulation.

33. Using NYSE seat prices as a measure of brokerage profitability, Schwert (1977) tested the hypothesis that the SEC is captured by the industry it regulates. He rejected that conclusion because of the decline in seat prices since the unfixing of commissions.

34. This $64,000 of course reflects the expected liquidation value of a seat (such as pro rata shares in real property) as well as the expected discounted profit stream of being a member. Thus the portion of the $64,000 that reflects the value of the NYSE as an ongoing business may be small, or even zero, since equity per member totaled $56,314 at the end of 1977 (see NYSE, 1978, p. 33).

35. The seat price experience should be distinguished from the evidence cited regarding stock prices of publicly traded firms. Exchange seat price experience and brokerage firm price performance may be independent since brokerage firms utilize both exchange- and nonexchange-trading facilities. Seat prices therefore may not be used to measure the economic welfare of public firms.

Chapter 5

1. See Lee A. Pickard, *The Money Manager* (November 26, 1979); *Wall Street Journal* (September 21, 1979).

2. Irwin Friend, *Activity on Over-the-Counter Markets* (Philadelphia, Pa.: University of Pennsylvania Press, 1951), pp. 13–16.

3. Robert Sobel, *Inside Wall Street* (New York: Norton, 1977).

4. James L. Hamilton, "Competition, Scale Economies, and Transactions Cost in the Stock Market," *Journal of Financial and Quantitative Analysis,* vol. 11 (1976), pp. 779–802.

5. U.S., Securities and Exchange Commission, *Report to the Commission by the Trading and Exchange Division on the Problem of Multiple Trading on Securities Exchanges* (Washington, D.C., November 20, 1940).

6. The 1934 Act required the SEC to begin collecting exchange volume data. Prior to that time, such data were unreliable.

7. Robert W. Doede, "The Monopoly Power of the New York Stock Exchange," Ph.D. dissertation, Department of Economics, The University of Chicago, 1967. Doede cited a working paper on this topic by Harold Demsetz in which lower spreads were associated with active securities. That study has since been published ("The Cost of Transacting," *Quarterly Journal of Economics,* vol. 82, 1968, pp. 33–53) and has been extended and substantiated by other authors. For example, see G. J. Benston and R. Hagerman, "Determinants of Bid-Ask Spreads in the Over-the-Counter Market," *Journal of Financial Economics,* vol. 1 (1974), pp. 353–364; S. M. Tinic and R. West, "Competition and the Pricing of Dealer Services in the Over-the-Counter Market," *Journal of Financial and Quantitative Analysis* (1972), p. 7; and Hans Stoll, "The Pricing of Security Dealer Services: An Empirical Study of NASDAQ Stocks," *Journal of Finance,* vol. 38 (1978), pp. 1153–1172.

8. See Geoge J. Stigler, "The Economics of Scale," *The Journal of Law and Economics,* vol. 1 (October 1958), pp. 54–71.

9. Doede, "The Monopoly Power," p. 41.

10. Ibid., p. 92.

11. G. William Schwert, "Public Regulation of National Securities Exchanges: A Test of the Capture Hypothesis," *Bell Journal of Economics* (spring 1977), pp. 128–150; and "Stock Exchange Seats as Capital Assets," *Journal of Financial Economics,* vol. 4 (1977), pp. 51–78.

12. Ibid., p. 53.

13. When contemporaneous and lagged returns were considered, however, seats exhibited more market risk than the common stock index (combined beta was greater than one).

14. Schwert, "Public Regulation," p. 143.

15. Schwert, "Public Regulation," p. 142.

16. Schwert, "Public Regulation," p. 147.

17. Consistent with the notion that the Amex has not been a competitor of the NYSE, the ratio of NYSE to Amex seat prices has been fairly constant since the late 1920s. Thus discussions relating the price behavior of the NYSE to that of the regionals could logically be extended to primary exchanges vs. the regionals. Returns to the Amex seatholders have followed a pattern similar to those of the NYSE seatholders.

18. Appendix A presents all holding period returns for these exchanges. These returns are calculated the same way as stock returns. See Roger G. Ibbotson and Rex A. Sinquefield, "Stocks, Bonds, Bills and Inflation: Year by Year Historical Returns (1926–1974)," *Journal of Business,* vol. 49 (January 1976), pp. 11–47.

19. The annual percentage price change of the NYSE seats for 1941 to 1944 was 19.4 percent and of the Phlx seats −18.4 percent (see appendix B).

20. Before 1935 the NYSE was the only source of estimated share volume. They estimate that reported share volume in 1920 was 227.6 million shares, compared to 207.6 million shares in 1940. The dollar volume was estimated to be $43,700 million in 1926 and $7,166 million in 1940 (NYSE *Fact Book for 1979,* p. 63).

21. This observation is consistent with the annual percentage price change for the exchanges from 1955 to 1974, −0.9 percent for NYSE and 1.6 percent for the Phlx.

22. Securities Exchange Act of 1934, sec. 11A(a)(2).

23. As an aside, there is no evidence that the consolidated tape has improved market efficiency, and thus it must be interpreted as a net cost imposed by the SEC (Kenneth D. Garbade and William C. Silber, "Technology, Communication, and the Performance of Financial Markets: 1840–1975," *Journal of Finance,* vol. 33, June 1978).

24. Peltzman, "Toward a More General," p. 224.

Chapter 6

1. "The SEC: Going Too Far Too Fast?" *Business Week* (November 27, 1978), p. 91.

2. Ibid., p. 86.

References

Bank and Stock Quotation Record, March 1950, 1955, 1960, 1965–1978.

Baxter, William F. "NYSE Fixed Commission Rates: A Private Cartel Goes Public." *Stanford Law Review,* vol. 22 (April 1970), pp. 675–712.

Federal Paperwork Commission. *A Report of the Commission on Federal Paperwork.* Final summary report, October 3, 1977.

Mann, Michael, "A Critique of the New York Stock Exchange's Report on the Economic Effects of Negotiated Commission Rates on the Brokerage Industry, the Market for Corporate Securities and the Investing Public." Prepared for the U.S. Department of Justice, October 1968.

Miller, James C., III. *Regulatory Reform: Some Problems and Approaches.* AEI reprint no. 72, August 1977.

National Association of Security Dealers. Letter from Richard B. Walbert, President NASD to U.S. Securities and Exchange Commission, April 1, 1968.

New York Stock Exchange. *1977 Annual Report,* 1978.

New York Stock Exchange. "Economic Effects of Negotiated Commissions on the Brokerage Industry, the Market for Corporate Securities, and the Investing Public," August 1968.

New York Stock Exchange. "The Economics of Minimum Commission Rates," May 1, 1969.

New York Stock Exchange. *Factbook,* various years.

New York Stock Exchange. "Public Transaction Study," 1976.

New York Stock Exchange. Letter from Robert W. Haack, president of the NYSE, January 2, 1968.

Peltzman, Sam. "Toward a More General Theory of Regulation." *Journal of Law and Economics,* vol. 19 (August 1976), pp. 211–240.

Rowen, H. A. "The Securities Acts Amendments of 1975: A Legislative History." *The Securities Law Journal* (winter 1976).

Schwert, William G. "Public Regulation of National Securities Exchanges: A Test of the Capture Hypothesis." *Bell Journal of Economics,* vol. 8 (spring 1977), pp. 128–150.

Silver v. New York Stock Exchange. 393 U.S. 341 (1963).

Stigler, George J. "The Theory of Economic Regulation." *Bell Journal of Economics and Management Science,* vol. 2 (1971).

Weidenbaum, Murray. *The New Wave of Government Regulation of Business.* AEI reprint no. 39, August 1976.

U.S., Congress, House, Subcommittee on Commerce and Finance. *Securities Industry Study.* Report of the Subcommittee on Commerce and Finance of the Committee on Interstate and Foreign Commerce. 93d Congress, 1st session, February 1973.

U.S. Congress, Senate, Subcommittee on Securities. *Securities Industry Study.* Interim Report of the Subcommittee on Securities of the Committee on Banking, Housing and Urban Affairs, 92d Congress, 2nd session, February 4, 1972.

U.S., Congress, Senate, Subcommittee on Securities. *Securities Industry Study.* Final Report of the Subcommittee on Securities to the Committee on Banking, Housing and Urban Affairs, 93d Congress, 1st session, February 1973.

U.S., Department of Justice. Comments submitted in response to the SEC release no. 8239, 1968.

U.S., Department of Justice. "Memorandum of the United States Department of Justice on the Fixed Minimum Commission Rate Structure." Statement submitted to the SEC, January 17, 1969.

U.S., Securities and Exchange Commission. *Industrial Investor Study Report.* Summary volume, March 1971.

U.S., Securities and Exchange Commission. Release no. 8239, January 26, 1968.

U.S., Securities and Exchange Commission. Release no. 8324, May 28, 1968.

U.S., Securities and Exchange Commission. Release no. 8860, April 2, 1970.

U.S., Securities and Exchange Commission. Release no. 9007, October 22, 1970.

U.S., Securities and Exchange Commission. Report of Special Study of Securities Markets, July 17, 1963, pp. 347, 350.

U.S., Securities and Exchange Commission. *Report to Congress on the Effect of the Absence of Fixed Commissions,* December 1, 1975, March 29, 1976, August 10, 1976, January 28, 1977, May 26, 1977.

U.S., Securities and Exchange Commission. Directorate of Economic and Policy Research. *Staff Report on the Securities Industry in 1977,* May 22, 1978.

Bibliography

Adams, Charles Francis, Jr. "Railroad Inflation." *North American Review*, vol. 108 (January 1969), pp. 163–164.

Adams, Charles Francis, Jr. "Boston I." *North American Review*, vol. 106 (January 1968), pp. 25.

Alchian, Armen A. "Information Costs, Pricing and Resource Unemployment." In *Microeconomic Foundations of Employment and Inflation Theory*, edited by Phelps, et al. New York: Norton, 1970.

Bank and Stock Quotation Record, New York: William B. Dana Co., March 1950, 1955, 1960, 1965–1978.

Baxter, William F. "NYSE Fixed Commission Rates: A Private Cartel Goes Public." *Stanford Law Review*, vol. 22 (April 1970), pp. 675–712.

Beaver, William H. "Current Trends in Corporate Disclosure." *Journal of Accountancy* (January 1978), pp. 44–52.

Beaver, William H. "The Reporting Responsibility of the SEC." *Financial Executive* (March 1977), pp. 14–19.

Beaver, William H. "The Implications of Security Price Research for Disclosure Policy and Analyst Community." Duke Second Accounting Symposium, December 2–3, 1976. In *Financial Information Requirements for Security Analysts*, edited by A. Rashad Abdel-Chalik and Thomas Kelov, pp. 65–81.

Benson, Lee. *Merchants, Farmers, and Railroads: Railroad Regulation and New York Politics, 1850–1887*. Cambridge, Mass.: Harvard University Press, 1955, pp. 212, 245.

Bernstein, Marver H. *Regulating Business by Independent Commission*. Princeton, N.J.: Princeton University Press, 1955.

Benston, George J. "Public (U.S.) Compared to Private (U.K.) Regulation of Corporate Financial Disclosure." *The Accounting Review*, vol. 11 (July 1976), pp. 483–498.

Benston, George J. "Accounting Standards in the United States and the United Kingdom: Their Nature, Causes and Consequences." *Vanderbilt Law Review*, vol. 28 (January 1975), pp. 235–268.

Benston, George J. "Financial Reporting of the Stock Market: Evaluation of the Securities Exchange Act of 1934" (followed by "The Other Side," by A. A. Sommer, Jr., Commissioner, SEC) and "Comments on 'The Other Side'." *Financial Executive*. Special issue on *Finance Reporting and the Stock Market* (May 1974), pp. 2–16, 28–42.

Benston, George J. "A Critique of the Rationale for Required Corporate Financial Disclosure." *The Emanuel Safe Distinguished Lectures in Accounting* (1973–1974), pp. 36–52.

Benston, George J. "Required Disclosure and the Stock Market: An Evaluation of the Securities Exchange Act of 1934." *American Economic Review*, vol. 63 (March 1973), pp. 132–155.

Black, Fischer. "Towards a Fully Automated Stock Exchange." *Financial Analysts Journal*, pt. 1, vol. 27 (July–August 1971), p. 29, pt. 2, vol. 27 (November-December 1971), p. 25.

Born, Rosco C. "Which Way Regulation?" Interview with Philip Loomis, SEC Commissioner. *Barrons* (May 28, 1979), p. 4 et seq.

Branch, Ben. "Deregulation and Price Competition in the Securities Industry: It Takes More than 'Benign Neglect,'" *Antitrust Law and Economics,* vol. 10 (1978), pp. 67–73.

Caine, Stanley P. *The Myth of a Progressive Reform: Railroad Regulation in Wisconsin 1903–1910.* Madison: State Historical Society of Wisconsin, 1970.

Cochran, Thomas C. *Railroad Leaders 1845–1890: The Business Mind in Action.* Cambridge, Mass.: Harvard University Press, pp. 189–199.

Cox, Edward F., et al. *"The Nader Report" on the Federal Trade Commission.* New York: R. W. Baron, 1969.

Davis, G. Cullom. "The Transformation of the Federal Trade Commission, 1914–1929." *Mississippi Valley Historical Review,* vol. 49 (December 1962), pp. 452ff.

De Bedts, Ralph F. *The New Deal's SEC: The Formative Years.* New York: Columbia University Press, 1964.

Dhaliwal, Dan S. "The Impact of Disclosure Regulations on the Cost of Capital." In *Economic Consequences of Financial Accounting Standards.* FASB research report, July 1978.

Doede, Robert. *The Monopoly Power of The New York Stock Exchange.* Ph.D. dissertation, The University of Chicago, June 1967.

Douglas, William O. *Yale Law Review* (1933) pp. 532–534.

Eastman, Joseph B. ICC Docket No. 22876, May 4, 1931. Eastman Papers, Robert Frost Library, Amherst College, Amherst, Mass.

Fama, Eugene F. "Efficient Capital Markets: A Review of Theory and Empirical Work." *Journal of Finance,* vol. 25 (May 1970), pp. 338–417.

Fama, Eugene F. "Agency Problems and the Theory of the Firm." Working paper series no. MERC 78-10, Graduate School of Management, The University of Rochester, November 1978.

Farrar, Donald E. "Toward A Central Market System: Wall Street's Slow Retreat into the Future." *Journal of Financial and Quantitative Analysis* (November 1974), pp. 815–828.

Farrar, Donald E. "The Martin Report: Wall Street's Proposed 'Great Leap Backward,'" *Financial Analysts Journal,* vol. 27 (September–October 1971), pp. 14–18.

Federal Paperwork Commission. *A Report of the Commission on Federal Paperwork.* Final summary report, October 3, 1977.

Fellmeth, Robert. *The Interstate Commerce Commission.* New York: Grossman Publishers, 1970.

Fisher, L., and J. H. Zorrie. "Some Studies of the Variability of Returns in Investments in Common Stock." *Journal of Business* (April 1970), pp. 99–134.

Flathman, Richard E. *The Public Interest: An Essay Concerning the Normative Discourse of Politics.* New York: Wiley, 1966.

Friedrich, Carl J., ed. *The Public Interest.* New York: Nomos V, Atherton Press, 1962.

Friend, Irwin. "Economic Foundations of Stock Market Regulation." Wharton School working paper no. 4-75, The University of Pennsylvania, June 23, 1975.

Friend, Irwin. *Activity of Over-the-Counter Markets.* Philadelphia: University of Pennsylvania Press, 1951.

Friend, Irwin and Edward S. Herman. "Professor Stigler on Securities' Regulation: A Further Comment." *Journal of Business,* vol. 38 (January 1965), pp. 106–110.

Friend, Irwin, and Edward S. Herman. "The SEC through a Glass Darkly." *Journal of Business* (October 1964), pp. 382–405.

Garfield, Paul J., and Wallace F. Lovejoy. *Public Utility Economics.* Englewood Cliffs, N.J.: Prentice-Hall, 1964.

Gonedes, Nicholas J., and Nicholas Dopuch. "Capital Market Equilibrium, Information Production, and Review of Empirical Work." *Market Equilibrium and Accounting Techniques; Studies on Financial Accounting Objectives* (1974), p. 48.

Graham, Otis L., Jr., ed. *From Roosevelt to Roosevelt: American Politics and Diplomacy 1901–1941.* New York: Appleton-Century-Crofts, 1971, pp. 70–109.

Green, Mark J. *The Monopoly Makers.* New York: Grossman Publishers, 1973.

Green, Mark J. *The Closed Enterprise System.* New York: Grossman Publishers, 1972.

Hamburg, Morris, Stanley Schor, and Winn Willis. *Characteristics of Transactions on Over-The-Counter Markets.* Philadelphia: The University of Pennsylvania Press, 1953.

Hamilton, James C. "Competition, Scale Economics and Transactions Cost in the Stock Market." *Journal of Financial and Quantitative Analysis,* vol. 11 (1976), pp. 779–802.

Harbeson, Robert U. "Railroads and Regulation, 1877–1916, Conspiracy or Public Interest?" *Journal of Economic History,* vol. 27 (June 1967), pp. 230–242.

Heilbroner, Robert, et al. *In the Name of Profits.* Garden City, N.Y.: Doubleday, 1972.

Held, Virginia. *The Public Interest and Individual Interests.* New York: Basic Books, 1970.

Hilton, George W. "The Basic Behavior of Regulatory Commissions." *American Economic Review,* vol. 62 (May 1972), pp. 47–54.

Hilton, George W. "The Consistency of the Interstate Commerce Act." *Journal of Law and Economics* vol. 9 (October 1966), pp. 87ff.

Hoffman, G. Wright. *Character and Extent of Over-The-Counter Markets.* Philadelphia: The University of Pennsylvania Press, 1952.

Horwitz, Bertrand, and Richard Kolodny. "Line of Business Reporting and Security Prices: An Analysis of an SEC Disclosure Rule." *Bell Journal of Economics,* vol. 8 (spring 1977), pp. 234–249.

Huntington, Samuel P. "The Marasmus of the ICC: The Commission, the Railroads, and the Public Interest." *Yale Law Journal,* vol. 41 (April 1952), pp. 467–509.

Ibbotson, Roger B., and Rex A. Sinquefield. "Stocks, Bonds, Bills and Inflation: Year-by-Year Historical Returns (1926–1974)." *The Journal of Business,* vol. 49 (January 1976), pp. 11–47.

Jaffe, Louis L. "The Effective Limits of the Administrative Process: A Reevaluation," *Harvard Law Review,* vol. 47 (May 1954), pp. 1105–1135.

Jensen, Michael C., and William H. Meckling. "Theory of the Firm: Managerial Behavior, Agency Costs and Ownership Structure," *Journal of Financial Economics,* vol. 3 (1976), pp. 305–360.

Jordan, William A. "Producer Protection, Prior Market Structure and Effects of Government Regulation." *Journal of Law and Economics,* vol. 15 (April 1972), pp. 151–176.

Kerr, K. Austin. *American Railroad Politics*. 1914–1920. Pittsburgh: University of Pittsburgh Press, 1968.

Kirkland, Edward Chase. *Men, Cities and Transportation: A Study in New England History, 1820–1900,* 2 vols. Cambridge, Mass.: Harvard University Press, 1948.

Kohlmeier, Louis M., Jr. *The Regulators: Watchdog Agencies and the Public Interest*. New York: Harper and Row, 1969.

Kolko, Gabriel. *Railroads and Regulation 1877–1916*. Princeton, N.J.: Princeton University Press, 1965.

Kolko, Gabriel. *The Triumph of Conservatism: A Reinterpretation of American History, 1900–1916*. New York: Free Press of Glencoe, 1963.

Kripke, Homer. *The SEC and Corporate Disclosure: Regulation in Search of a Purpose*. New York: Harcourt Brace Jovanovich, 1979.

Landis, James Macauley. "Report on Regulatory Agencies to the President-Elect." U.S., Senate, Committee on the Judiciary, 86th Congress, 2d session, 1960.

Landis, James Macauley. *The Administrative Process*. New Haven, Conn.: Yale University Press, 1938.

Leuchtenburg, William E. "The Case of the Contentious Commissioner: Humphrey's Executor v. U.S." In *Freedom and Reform: Essays in Honor of Henry Steele Commager*. Harold M. Hyman and Leonard W. Levy, eds. New York: Harper and Row, 1967.

Loomis, Carol J. "The Shakeout on Wall Street Isn't Over Yet," *Fortune,* May 22, 1978, pp. 59–66.

MacAvoy, Paul W. "The Regulation-Induced Shortage of Natural Gas." *Journal of Law and Economics,* vol. 14 (April 1971), pp. 167–199.

MacAvoy, Paul W., ed. *The Crisis of the Regulatory Commissions*. New York: Norton, 1970.

Mahon, Gigi. "Judge and Jury: An Authority on Civil Liberties Looks at the SEC." *Barron's,* February 21, 1977, pp. 3–5.

Mann, Michael. "A Critique of the New York Stock Exchange's Report on the Economic Effects of Negotiated Commission Rates on the Brokerage Industry, the Market for Corporate Securities and the Investing Public." Prepared for the U.S. Department of Justice, October 1968.

Manne, Henry G. *The Economics of Legal Relationships; Readings in the Theory of Property Rights*. St. Paul, Minn.: West Publishing Co., 1975.

Manne, Henry G., ed. *Economic Policy and the Regulation of Corporate Securities*. Conference proceedings. Washington, D.C.: American Enterprise Institute for Public Policy Research, 1969.

Manne, Henry G. *Insider Trading and the Stock Market*. New York: Free Press, 1966.

Martin, Albro. "Enterprise Denied, Passim; 'The Troubled Subject of Railroad Regulation in the Gilded Age—A Reappraisal.'" *Journal of American History,* vol. 41 (September 1974), pp. 339–371.

Martin, Albro. *Enterprise Denied: Origins of the Decline of American Railroads, 1897–1917*. New York: Columbia University Press, 1971.

Martin, William M., Jr. "The Securities Markets, a Report, with Recommendations. Submitted to the Board of Governors of the NYSE," August 5, 1971.

McKie, James W. "Regulation and the Free Market: The Problem of Boundaries." *Bell Journal of Economics and Management Science,* vol. 1 (spring 1970), pp. 6–26.

Miller, George H. *Railroads and the Granger Laws.* Madison: University of Wisconsin Press, 1971.

Miller III, James C. *Regulatory Reform: Some Problems and Approaches.* AEI reprint no. 72, August 1977.

Moore, Thomas G. *Freight Transportation Regulation: Surface Freight and the Interstate Commerce Commission.* Washington, D.C., 1972.

Nash, Gerald D. "Origins of the Interstate Commerce Act of 1887." *Pennsylvania History,* vol. 24 (July 1957), pp. 181–190.

National Association of Security Dealers. *The NASDAQ/OTC Market Statistical Review.* New York, 1971–1976.

National Association of Security Dealers. *The NASDAQ/OTC Securities Fact Book.* New York, various years.

National Association of Security Dealers. Letter from Richard B. Walbert, president of the NASD to the Securities and Exchange Commission, April 1, 1968.

Noll, Roger. *Reforming Regulation.* Washington, D.C.: The Brookings Institution, 1971.

New York Stock Exchange. *1977 Annual Report on the NYSE.* New York, 1978.

New York Stock Exchange. "The Economics of Minimum Commission Rates." New York, May 1, 1969.

New York Stock Exchange. "Economic Effects of Negotiated Commissions on the Brokerage Industry, the Market for Corporate Securities, and the Investing Public." New York, August 1968.

New York Stock Exchange. *NYSE Factbook.* New York, various years.

New York Stock Exchange. "Public Transaction Study." New York, 1957, 1961–1970, 1971, 1974, 1976.

New York Stock Exchange. Letter from Robert W. Haack, president of the NYSE, January 2, 1968.

Peltzman, Sam. "Toward a More General Theory of Regulation." *Journal of Law and Economics,* vol. 19 (August 1976), pp. 211–240.

Phillips, Almarin, ed. *Promoting Competition in Regulated Markets,* Washington, D.C.: The Brookings Institution, 1975.

Phillips, C. F. *The Economics of Regulation,* Homewood: Richard D. Irwin, Inc., 1969.

Pickard, Lee A. "The National Market System: 'A Will-O'-The Wisp.'" *The Money Manager,* vol. 8 (November 26, 1979).

Posner, Richard A. *Economic Analysis of the Law.* 2nd ed. Boston: Little, Brown, 1977.

Posner, Richard A. "Theories of Economic Regulation." *Bell Journal of Economics and Management Science* vol. 5 (autumn 1974), pp. 335–358.

Posner, Richard A. "Taxation by Regulation." *Bell Journal of Economics and Management Science,* no. 2 (1971).

Purcell, Jr., Edward A. "Ideas and Interests: Businessmen and the Interstate Commerce Act." *Journal of American History,* vol. 54 (December 1967), pp. 561–578.

Report of the President's Commission of Financial Structure and Regulation ("The Hunt Report"), December, 1971.

Roll, Richard. "A Critique of the Cost Pricing Theory's Test, Part 1: On Past and Potential Testability of the Theory." *Journal of Financial Economics,* vol. 4 (March 1, 1977), pp. 129–176.

Robbins, Sidney, and Werner, Walter. "Professor Stigler Revisited." *Journal of Business,* vol. 37 (October 1964), pp. 414–422.

Rowen, Harvey A. "The Securities Acts Amendments of 1975: A Legislative History." *Securities Regulation Law Journal,* vol. 3 (1976), pp. 329–346.

Saari, Christopher Paul. "The Efficient Capital Market Hypothesis, Economic Theory and the Regulation of the Securities Industry." *Stanford Law Review,* vol. 28 (May 1977), pp. 1031–1076.

Salmanowitz, John M. "Broker Investment Recommendations and the Efficient Market Hypothesis: A Proposed Cautionary Legend." *Stanford Law Review,* vol. 29 (May 1977), p. 1077.

Scheiber, Harry N. "The Road to Munn: Eminent Domain and the Concept of Public Purpose in the State Courts." *Perspectives in American History,* vol. 5 (1971), pp. 327–402.

Schmalensee, Richard. *The Control of Natural Monopolies.* Lexington, Mass.: Lexington Books, 1979.

Schmidt, Seymour. "Which Road to an Efficient Stock Market—Free Competition or Regulated Monopoly?" *Financial Analysts Journal,* vol. 27 (September–October, 1971), p. 18.

Schubert, Glendon. *The Public Interest.* Glencoe, Ill.: Free Press, 1960.

Schwert, William G. "Measuring the Effects of Regulation: Evidence from Capital Markets." Working paper series no. APB 78-7. Center for Research in Government Policy and Business, University of Rochester, October 1978.

Schwert, William G. "Stock Exchange Seats as Capital Assets." *Journal of Financial Economics,* vol. 4 (1977), pp. 51–78.

Schwert, William G. "Public Regulation of National Securities Exchanges: A Test of the Capture Hypothesis." *Bell Journal of Economics,* vol. 8 (spring 1977), pp. 128–150.

"The SEC: Going Too Far Too Fast?" *Business Week,* November 27, 1978, pp. 86–92.

Silver v. New York Stock Exchange. 393 U.S. 341 (1963).

Skousen, K. Fred. *An Introduction to the SEC.* 2nd ed. Cincinnati: South-Western Publishing Co., 1980.

Sobel, Robert. *Inside Wall Street.* New York: Norton, 1977.

Sobel, Robert. *The Great Bull Market.* New York: Norton, 1968.

Sobel, Robert. *NYSE: A History of the New York Stock Exchange 1935–1975.* New York: Weybright and Talley, 1975.

Stigler, George J. "Comment." *Journal of Business* (October 1964), pp. 414–422.

Stigler, George J. "The Economics of Scale." *The Journal of Law and Economics* vol. 1 (October 1958), pp. 54–71.

Stigler, George J. "Public Regulation of Securities Markets." *Journal of Business,* vol. 37 (April 1964), p. 117.

Stigler, George J. "The Theory of Economic Regulation." *Bell Journal of Economics and Management Science,* vol. 3 (1971).

Stigler, George J. "The SEC through a Glass Darkly." *Journal of Business* vol. 37 (October 1964), pp. 414–422.

Stigler, George J. and Claire Friedland. "What Can Regulators Regulate?" The Case of Electricity." *Journal of Law and Economics,* vol. 5 (October 1962), pp. 1–16.

Stillman, Stanley. "Wall Street vs. the SEC: The Battle Goes On." *Financial Executive* (April 1975), pp. 28–30.

Stoll, Hans R. "Regulation of Securities Markets: An Examination of the Effects of Increased Competition." Solomon Brothers Center for the Study of Financial Institutions Monograph, 1979-2, New York University, 1979.

Stone, James H. *One Way for Wall Street: A View of the Future of the Securities Industry.* Boston: Little, Brown, 1975.

U.S., Congress, House Committee on Interstate and Foreign Commerce. *Report of the Advisory Committee on Corporate Disclosure to the Securities and Exchange Commission.* 95th Congress, 1st session. Committee Print 95-29. Washington, D.C.: Government Printing Office, Nov. 3, 1977.

U.S., Congress, House Committee on Interstate and Foreign Commerce. *Institutional Investor Study Report of the Securities and Exchange Commission.* 92nd Congress, 1st session. House Document No. 92-64. Washington, D.C.: Government Printing Office, 1971.

U.S., Congress, House Subcommittee on Commerce and Finance. *Securities Industry Study.* Report of the Subcommittee on Commerce and Finance of the Committee on Interstate and Foreign Commerce. 93rd Congress, 1st session. Washington, D.C.: Government Printing Office, February 1973.

U.S., Congress, Senate Subcommittee on Securities. *Securities Industry Study.* Interim report of the Subcommittee on Securities of the Committee on Banking, Housing, and Urban Affairs. 92nd Congress, 2nd session. Washington, D.C.: Government Printing Office, February 4, 1972.

U.S., Congress, Senate. *Securities Industry Study.* Final report of the Subcommittee on Securities to the Committee on Banking, Housing, and Urban Affairs. 93rd Congress, 1st session. Washington, D.C.: Government Printing Office, February 1973.

U.S., Department of Justice. Comments submitted in response to the Securities and Exchange Commission's release no. 8239 (1968).

U.S., Department of Justice. "Memorandum of the United States Department of Justice on the Fixed Minimum Commission Rate Structure." Statement submitted to the Securities and Exchange Commission, January 17, 1969.

U.S., Securities and Exchange Commission. *Directory of Companies Required to File Annual Reports with the SEC under the Securities Act of 1934,* June 30, 1976.

U.S., Securities and Exchange Commission. *Institutional Investor Study Report.* Summary volume (March 1971).

U.S., Securities and Exchange Commission. *News Digest.*

U.S. Securities and Exchange Commission. "Policy Statement of the Securities and Exchange Commission on the Structure of a Central Market System," March 29, 1973.

U.S., Securities and Exchange Commission. "Reports of the Advisory Committee on the Implementation of a Central Market System" ("The Yearly Committee Report"), September 12, 1975.

U.S., Securities and Exchange Commission. Release no. 8239 (January 26, 1968).

U.S., Securities and Exchange Commission. Release no. 8324 (May 28, 1968).

U.S., Securities and Exchange Commission. Release no. 8860 (April 2, 1970).

U.S., Securities and Exchange Commission. Release no. 9007 (October 22, 1970).

U.S., Securities and Exchange Commission. Report of special study of securities markets (July 17, 1963), 347, 350.

U.S., Securities and Exchange Commission. *Report to the Commission by the Trading and Exchange Division on the Problem of Multiple Trading on Securities Exchanges.* Washington, D.C., November 20, 1940.

U.S., Securities and Exchange Commission. *Report to Congress on the Effect of the Absence of Fixed Commissions.* December 1, 1975, March 29, 1976, August 10, 1976, January 28, 1977, May 26, 1977.

U.S., Securities and Exchange Commission. Directorate of Economic and Policy Research. *Staff Report on the Securities Industry in 1977.* May 22, 1978, July 26, 1979.

U.S., Securities and Exchange Commission. *Statistical Bulletin.* Various years.

Verschaur, Jack. "Negotiated Commissions in the Securities Industry. An Analysis of Fee Changes after May 1, 1975." Paper Presented at Midwest Finance Association, Chicago, Ill., March 1979.

Volner, Ian D. "Getting the Horse Before the Cart: Identifying the Causes of Failure of the Regulatory Commissions." *Hofstra Law Review,* vol. 5 (winter 1977), pp. 285–313.

Watts, Ross L., and Zimmerman, Jerold L. "The Demand for and Supply of Accounting Theories, The Market for Excuses." Working paper no. GPB 77-7. Graduate School of Management, The University of Rochester, January 1978.

Watts, Ross L. "Corporate Financial Statements, A Product of the Market and Political Processes." *Australian Journal of Management,* vol. 2 (April 1977), pp. 53–75.

Weidenbaum, Murray L. "Four Questions for OSHA." *Labor Law Journal,* vol. 30 (August 1979), pp. 528–531.

Weidenbaum, Murray L. *The New Wave of Government Regulation of Business.* AEI reprint no. 39 (August 1976).

Welles, Chris. "Wall Street's Last Gold Mine." *Institutional Investor* (February 1978), pp. 34–79.

Welles, Chris. *The Last Days of the Club.* New York: Dutton, 1975.

West, Richard R., and Seha M. Tinic. *The Economics of the Stock Market.* New York: Praeger, 1971.

West, Richard R. "Brokers' Fortune Since 'May Day'." *Wall Street Journal* (November 24, 1978).

Williamson, D. E. *The Economics of Discretionary Behavior: Management in a Theory of the Firm.* Englewood Cliffs, N.J.: Prentice-Hall, 1964.

Wilson, James Q. "The Dead Hand of Regulation." *The Public Interest,* vol. 25 (fall 1971), pp. 46–49.

Index

Accounting, 7
Advisory Committee on Corporate Disclosure to the Securities and Exchange Commission, 27–28, 30, 36, 43, 113
Amendments to the 1934 Act, 3, 14–15, 91, 108
Amex (American Stock Exchange), 13, 56, 85, 97, 100–101, 103
Anheuser-Busch, 95
Antitrust legislation, 6–7, 58, 87
ASE (American Stock Exchange). See Amex
Ash, Roy L., 20
Automatic execution systems, 107

Barter, 80
Benston, George, J., 32–33, 35, 38
Best execution rule, 108
Blue sky laws, 6–8
Budge, Hamer, 14
Buttonwood Tree Agreement, 6, 114

Carter, Jimmy, 15
Cary, William, 14
Casey, William J., 14
CFTC (Commodities Futures Trading Commission), 110, 119
Chapter IX Bankruptcy legislation, 12
Chicago Board of Trade, 117
Chicago Board Options Exchange, 117
Cohen, Manuel, 14, 57
Cohen, Milton, 14
COMEX, 107
Commission rates, 80, 103
  cost, 72
  deregulation of, 6, 15, 102, 105, 111, 115
  estimated competitive commission cost, 79
  fixed, 3, 6, 15, 23, 53, 55, 60, 84, 87
  individual rates, 67, 69, 72
  institutional rates, 67, 69, 72
  negotiated, 58, 60
  schedule, 65, 67
Congress, 88, 115
Connecticut General Insurance, 95
Consent decree, 111
Cook, G. Bradford, 14

Coolidge, Calvin, 11
Corporate governance, 119
Cost-benefit test, 44
CSE (Cincinnati Stock Exchange), 108, 109

Deregulation, 53
Disclosure
  corporate, 3, 7, 9, 15, 27, 111–112, 114, 119
  mandated, 42
  SEC system of, 42, 44
Doede, Robert W., 100, 107, 116
Douglas, William O., 12–13, 15, 30, 37

Economic efficiency, 17, 29
Economics of regulation, 3
Enforcement division, SEC, 14
Equity Funding, 19, 111
Exchanges, 85

FASB (Financial Accounting Standards Board), 112
Federal Reserve Board, 10, 110
Ford, Gerald R., 14
Fourth market, 80
Fraud, 7
Friend, Irwin, 34, 93
FTC (Federal Trade Commission), 9–11
Futures, commodity, 92, 110

Garrett, Ray, 14
GNMA, 119
Gray, William A., 30

Haack, Robert, 56–57
Healy, Robert E., 10–11
Herman, Edward S., 34
Hills, Roderick, 1, 14–15
Hoover, Herbert, 8
Hyatt Corporation, 95

Individual investors, 89
Individual trading, 65, 88
Insider trading, 36
Institutional investors, 23, 89
Institutional Investor Study Report, 59
Institutional trading, 65

Investment Advisors Act of 1940, 11
Investment Company Act of 1940, 11
ITS (Intermarket Trading Systems), 108

Jensen, Michael, 38
Johnson, Lyndon B., 14
Justice Department, 57–58, 87–88, 102, 109

Kennedy, John F., 13–14
Kennedy, Joseph, 10–12, 15
Kripke, Homer, 21, 27, 112

Landis, James M., 10, 12, 14–15
Line-of-business accounting. *See* Segmental accounting
London Stock Exchange, 101
Loss, Louis, 120

Malony Act, 11
Management perks, 28
Manipulation, stock price, 7
Mann, Michael, 58
Market failure, 17–18
Market model, 31
Martin, William M., 59
Matthews, George M., 10
MAX, 107
Meckling, William, 38
MSE (Midwest Stock Exchange), 100, 107
Monitoring expenditures, 40
Multiple Trading Case, 97
Mutual funds, 56

NASD (National Association of Securities Dealers), 7, 56, 108
NASDAQ (National Association of Securities Dealers Automated Quotation System), 86, 94, 103
National market system, 3, 6, 15, 91
Natural monopoly, 107–108
New York City bond problems, 119
Nixon, Richard M., 14
Noll, Roger, 20
Nonprice competition, 80
NYSE (New York Stock Exchange), 6, 8, 12, 38, 53, 55–60, 62, 64–65, 79–80, 83, 85, 87, 89, 92, 96, 100–101, 103, 105, 107, 109, 114–118
NYSE Rule 390, 108, 118

Open Board of Stock Brokers, 97
Options, 15, 91, 108–110
OTC (Over-the-Counter), 11, 55–56, 85, 92, 94, 103
Overseas payments, 28

PACE, 107
Pecora, Ferdinand, 10
Peltzman, Sam, 17, 61–63, 79–80, 83, 88–89, 109
Penn Central, 119
Phlx (Philadelphia Stock Exchange), 100, 104–105, 107, 117
Production function, 79
PSE (Pacific Stock Exchange), 100, 107
Public choice, 17, 21–22
Public Utility Holding Company Act of 1935, 11
Public utility holding companies, 7, 111
Public utilities, 11
Put and Call Dealers Association, 7

RAM (Regional Automated Market), 108. *See also* WHAM
Regional stock exchanges, 56, 80, 85, 97, 103–105, 107–109, 117
Regulatory tax
  for individuals, 72
  for institutions, 72
  NYSE, 79
Replacement cost accounting, 28
RMS (Regional Market System). *See* RAM
Roosevelt, Franklin D., 5, 9–10
Roper, Daniel C., 9

SAFECO, 95
Schmalensee, Richard, 20
Schwert, G. William, 101–103, 105, 107, 117
SEC (Securities and Exchange Commission), 11–12, 56–60, 64, 80, 83, 87–89, 91, 97, 102–103, 108–109, 112, 114–120
SEC disclosure forms
  10-K, 28, 32, 37, 43–44, 46, 49, 113
  10-Q, 28, 32, 43–44, 46, 49, 113
  8-K, 28, 32, 43–44, 46, 49, 113
  S-1, 28, 43, 46, 48, 113–114
  S-7, 28, 43, 46, 48, 113
  S-14, 28, 43, 46, 48, 113
  S-16, 28, 43, 46, 48, 114

Securities Act of 1933 (1933 act), 9–10, 12, 17, 38
Securities Act Amendments of 1964, 14
Securities Exchange Act of 1934 (1934 act), 10, 12, 14, 32, 38, 58–60, 91, 102
Securities industry, 91
Segmental accounting, 28
Self-regulation, 1, 7
Senate Banking and Currency Committee, 10
Sherman Antitrust laws, 6, 7, 58, 87
Silver v. New York Stock Exchange, 58
SIPA (Securities Investor Protection Act), 14, 59
SIPC (Securities Investor Protection Corporation), 14
Small firms, 114
Sobel, Robert, 5
Social benefits, 29
Social cost, 29
Sommers, Albert A., 15
Sporkin, Stanley, 14
Stigler, George E., 33–34, 61, 63, 79–80, 88–89, 100
Subsidy, 69
Supreme Court, 13

Third market, 14, 80, 86, 108, 119
Transaction cost, 65. *See also* Commission rates
Treasury Department, 110
Trust Indenture Act of 1939, 11

Weeden and Company, 86
WHAM (Weeden Holding Company Automated Market), 108. *See also* RAM
Whitney, Richard, 8, 12
Widows and orphans, 2
Williams, Harold, 15